Finding Fulfillment

ON LIFE'S UNCERTAIN SEAS

The Book of Ephesians

DOROTHY DAVIS

REGULAR BAPTIST PRESS
1300 North Meacham Road
Schaumburg, Illinois 60173-4806

In Dedication

To my mother-in-law, Alice,
with gratitude for your labor of love at the computer
and your encouragement of my writing ministry.

FINDING FULFILLMENT ON LIFE'S UNCERTAIN SEAS

© 2000

Regular Baptist Press • Schaumburg, Illinois

www.regularbaptistpress.org • 1-800-727-4440

Printed in U.S.A.

RBP5245 • ISBN: 978-0-87227-206-4

Third printing: 2007

Contents

Preface

As this tiny sapphire sphere called Earth spins in the vast blackness of space, the human specks that scurry upon it often pause, look up at the myriad of stars, and ponder ancient questions: What is life all about? Why am I here? Since the dawn of creation, man has desired to understand his significance, to know the reason he exists. The human heart must have a goal in life if it is to have a sense of worth.

In our society today, human beings often feel like frail, battered vessels adrift on a thrashing sea of confusion and despair. Surrounded by a shadowy mist, they seek a desirable land called "Fulfillment," but between them and this land are the hidden rocks of rejection, insignificance, and failure. To many people it seems hopeless to steer a course safely into the harbor of fulfillment without becoming shipwrecked on these treacherous rocks. And many people chart a course that seems right, such as the way of wealth, the way of fame, or the way of pleasure, only to end up sinking into an empty void.

But there is a way! Can't you see it? The sure, steady light of God's Truth shines a path through the dangers of life's uncertain seas. If we follow that light, we will come ultimately to fulfillment and step on shore with joy and a great sense of satisfaction.

The New Testament book of Ephesians discusses vital issues that pertain to the human problems of rejection, insignificance, and failure. As we follow the light of God's Word, the Bible, we will see how to overcome these defeating feelings and live as women of worth—worth that is bestowed upon us by God Himself.

Introduction

Suppose you had just met a man and struck up a conversation with him. In the course of your discussion you learn that he had been reared in a cultured environment, had graduated in the top of his class in a renowned academic institution, and had become a determined, untiring worker in his profession, attaining recognition and accomplishment. No doubt you would have considered this man to be highly successful, living a fulfilled life. But you would have come to the wrong conclusion.

Actually, the man I just described lived about two thousand years ago, and his name was Saul of Tarsus, later called "the apostle Paul." You see, despite all his earthly attainments, this man was not fulfilled because he lacked a right relationship to God and a proper purpose in life. At the foundation of his life he was spiritually empty.

But one day he had an encounter with the Lord Jesus Christ. (You can read about it in Acts 9:1-19.) His whole life did a 180-degree turn. As Paul himself later expressed it, "But what things were gain to me, those I counted loss for Christ. Yea doubtless, and I count all things but loss for the excellency of the knowledge of Christ Jesus my Lord" (Philippians 3:7, 8). Paul had finally found true fulfillment—not in his own accomplishments, but in knowing his Lord and God and in doing His work. Paul died a fulfilled person, declaring, "I have fought a good fight, I have finished my course, I have kept the faith" (2 Timothy 4:7).

After putting his faith in the Lord Jesus Christ, Paul became a traveling missionary, starting churches of believers in cities all across the Roman Empire. One of these churches was in the city of Ephesus, in what is now the country of Turkey. Sometime later, about A.D. 60, Paul wrote a letter to these Ephesian Christians while he was in prison in Rome for preaching about Christ. The letter he wrote to them is the New Testament book of Ephesians, a book that encourages believers to live up to their rich heritage in Christ.

How to Use This Study

Each lesson in this study is divided into five sections. Follow these suggestions as you prepare each lesson.

I. SOUNDING THE DEPTHS OF YOUR HEART

Following the introductory comments, these questions will prepare your heart to study God's Word. The answers to these questions will not be discussed in class.

II. IN LIGHT OF THE SCRIPTURES

The questions in this section concentrate on the actual text of God's Word and will help you understand what God's Word says.

III. CHARTING YOUR COURSE

As you answer the questions in this section, you will see how the truths of God's Word apply to your life.

IV. DROP ANCHOR

This section is personal. It is designed as a starting point to help you put God's truth into practice.

V. STEPPING OUT ON FAITH

These final words will help seal firmly in your mind what you learned from the Bible passage.

Incredible Credentials

Ephesians 1:1-14

"According as he hath chosen us in him before the foundation of the world, that we should be holy and without blame before him in love" (Ephesians 1:4).

Rejection. It is a feeling that can cast the soul into utter despair. It is the devastation of a spouse's unfaithfulness, the betrayal of a friend, the scar in a child's heart because of a parent's lack of love. We fear rejection and crave the security of being wanted, loved, and cared for.

Hopefully, each of us has people in our lives who provide emotional security. Yet the perfect Father, the ever-faithful Friend, the Lover of our souls is God. The first chapter of Ephesians is overwhelming with astonishing spiritual truths. It is worthy of our serious study and meditation. The woman who personally receives these truths as her own will never need to fear total rejection, for God will always be there with open arms to receive and love her. She will live with the foundational knowledge of her own significance, a significance based on God's acceptance.

When we come to Him and become His daughters, He not only accepts us but also makes us heirs of all Christ's wealth. We now live with incredible credentials: children of God and joint-heirs with Jesus Christ of all God's riches!

I. SOUNDING THE DEPTHS OF YOUR HEART

• In your opinion, what are the most important credentials you have in life?

• How do these contribute to your value as a person?

II. IN LIGHT OF THE SCRIPTURES

Read Ephesians 1:1-14.

1. In the opening verses of Ephesians, the Scriptural spotlight shines on God the Father and His Son, the Lord Jesus Christ. The fountain of spiritual blessing that is about to overflow upon us springs from the Godhead. In verse 1, what two terms are used to describe believers in Christ? Of what might these phrases remind the reader?

2. What two gifts are the Father and the Son able to give to us according to verse 2?

3. In verse 3, what did Paul declare that God has done for us?

4. From where do these blessings originate? Why is this significant?

5. Paul went on to discuss these blessings more specifically. They cover the past, present, and future. In the ages past—before the earth was even created—God *knew* about each of us! He planned to bring us into being. What else did He do (vv. 4, 5)?

6. What reasons are mentioned in verses 4-6 as God's motivation for doing this?

7. According to verses 7 and 8, what benefits does a person receive when she is "in Christ"?

8. Verses 9 and 10 tell us of a mystery that God has revealed to us that will take place in the future. What is this mystery?

9. What is the ultimate purpose God has for having predestined and chosen us to be His own (vv. 11, 12)?

10. In verses 13 and 14 we are given a summary of *our* part in salvation. (Remember: God's part was choosing us, lavishing His grace upon us, and sending Christ to die for us so that we could have forgiveness of sin.) What are we to do?

11. What does God do the moment we receive Christ and the good news of salvation? Why does He do this (vv. 13, 14)?

III. CHARTING YOUR COURSE

1. Reread verses 1-14. What "picture" of God the Father does this passage develop in your mind? How does this enhance your sense of trust in Him and your ability to approach Him as your Heavenly Father?

2. Look up the word "adoption" in a Bible dictionary. (See also Galatians 4:4-7.) What does this word mean to you spiritually? How should this affect the way you live?

3. Look up the word "redemption." What does this mean to you spiritually? How should this affect the way you live?

4. The idea expressed in verses 11-14 is that we have received an inheritance along with Christ. What might this inheritance be? When will we fully receive it? (See also Romans 8:17 and 1 Peter 1:3-5.)

5. What are the reasons, stated several times in this passage, that God has done all these things on our behalf?

6. Explain how each of the following blessings makes you a woman of worth.

God's choosing you before the world began

God's sending His Son, the Lord Jesus, to die and shed His blood for your sins so that you could be redeemed from sin's slavery

God's adopting you into His family

God's sealing you with His Spirit as a guarantee of your inheritance with Christ

God's lavishing spiritual riches and blessings upon you by His grace

An Illustration to Examine: The Prodigal Son

Read Luke 15:11-32.

7. Describe the qualities of the father.

8. How might the son have experienced rejection?

9. Relate this parable to God's loving acceptance of you.

IV. DROP ANCHOR

How has God spoken to you through Ephesians 1:1-14?

___ God loved you and valued you so much that He sent His precious Son, Jesus Christ, to die on the cross and shed His blood for your sins (John 3:16). God has provided the only way that you can go to Heaven when you die. You cannot do anything to get yourself there. You must believe what God says and trust Him. Have you ever accepted Christ as your Savior and received forgiveness for your sins? If not, why not talk to Him in prayer right now? Ask Him to become your Savior. Ask God to adopt you as His daughter and bring you into His family through Christ. The best credential in life is to be one of God's children (John 1:12).

___ As one who has put her trust in Christ already, take an honest inventory of your life. Are you living as a pleasing, obedient daughter to your Heavenly Father? Are you placing a high value on the spiritual riches and grace He has for you? Is your life bringing praise and glory to Him? If not, ask Him today to teach you how to live a life that will please Him. As the Spirit points out areas in your life that God wants to change—habits, relationships, words, attitudes, thoughts—obey Him and commit yourself anew to live as one who will walk worthy of belonging to Him.

___ Do you feel as if God might not love you because you have failed Him in some way? What did you learn in this lesson that assures you that God loves you with no strings attached? We *never* merit His love and grace; He gives it to us because of the *merits of His Son.* Talk to God about how you feel, but focus your faith on what the Bible tells you about God's love for you. If you are "in Christ," God couldn't love you more!

___ Upon what are you placing your value as a human being: your looks, your abilities, your education, possessions, background, accomplishments, religious good works, moral life? The Bible declares that our value is based upon our relationship to God by faith, grace, and mercy. Begin to see this as your greatest asset and make it a personal daily priority to cultivate your relationship with God. When He is truly the Lord of your life, He will do great things in you, for you, and through you!

V. STEPPING OUT ON FAITH

Before a woman can find fulfillment in life, she must understand her own significance. Without God and the truth expressed in His Word, a woman will seek significance through a variety of sources that are, at best, unstable. She may depend on her appearance, but appearance can change. Perhaps she looks to her skills, but the demand for those skills may diminish. She could be counting on wealth, position, or possessions, but if adverse circumstances arise, all of these can disappear in a day.

Personal significance must have its foundation in that which is unalterable: God and His Word. If we base our worth on our relationship to Him, a relationship that cannot fall apart because of *His* faithfulness to us, we will have a solid foundation upon which we can build a successful life. All the other factors that make us "feel" significant may ebb and wane, but the mainstay of our personal value, God's acceptance, will securely support us.

God loves us and wants us to be His children. But the Bible declares that we are all sinners (Romans 3:23) and by our sin are spiritually separated from God. He sent His Son to earth to live, die an agonizing death as the punishment for our sins, and be raised from the tomb. All of this was for our benefit—so that through our putting our faith in Jesus Christ, God could forgive our sins, redeem us from Satan's control, and adopt us into His own spiritual family. He now cares for us and blesses us with abundant grace and spiritual wealth. And the best is yet to come!

Do you fear rejection? God will accept you in Christ. Once you come to Him, He'll never let you go. In this vessel of Christ's love, we set sail for the land of fulfillment!

A Provision of Power

Ephesians 1:15-23

"That the God of our Lord Jesus Christ, the Father of glory, may give unto you the spirit of wisdom and revelation in the knowledge of him" (Ephesians 1:17).

Many people have charted a course to fulfillment through the channel of power. Their goal is to have influence and recognition, be it in their corporation, among their peers, or in our society. Some seek power through money, some through position or fame. Many times the "heroes" of our day are those who have made it to the top of their field, yet their personal lives are shattered as a result of sin and failure. In spite of this, many people—even Christians—envy their place of power and influence.

For the disciple of the Lord Jesus Christ, the word "power" should always direct our thoughts back to God, the only One Who truly has power. Think of the most influential man or woman you know. In God's eyes that person is but a vapor that will vanish (James 4:14). But our God is infinite in power (Psalm 135:5, 6), and He is willing to impart His power to us, His children, as we need it.

God's power is not worldly power, but spiritual power that will assure us of a successful life. The worldly woman grasps after the mirage of power to control her own life, but a righteous woman yields herself to God's power and finds her true source of satisfaction and strength. Because of our position in Christ, we can obtain this power through prayer and total dependence upon Him.

Lacking power? God has promised to provide it for you through Christ, your provision of power.

I. SOUNDING THE DEPTHS OF YOUR HEART

• Right now do you desire God to be in complete control of your life, including your thoughts, attitudes, words, and actions?

• At some time since you received Christ as Savior, did you commit total control of your life to the Lord Jesus Christ?

II. IN LIGHT OF THE SCRIPTURES

Read Ephesians 1:15-23.

1. The Ephesian believers already had a degree of spiritual maturity. As their spiritual caretaker, Paul saw areas that they needed to deepen. What two spiritual qualities did they already have (v. 15)?

2. What did Paul ask the Father to give them (v. 17)?

3. In what would this result (v. 17)?

4. In verses 18 and 19, for what three things did Paul ask the Ephesians to know and understand?

5. In verse 18, to what part of your being might "the eyes of your understanding" refer? Is it mental, spiritual, emotional, physical, or any combination of these?

6. Paul focused on God's power in verses 19 and 20. The same power that works in us also did what two things?

7. Read verse 21. Describe Christ's position in your own words.

8. What description of Christ is given in relation to His church (v. 22)?

9. What description of the church is given in relation to Christ (v. 23)?

10. Review this passage again. How is the portrayal of the Lord Jesus in these verses different from the way we usually think of Him?

III. CHARTING YOUR COURSE

Looking at this passage in another way, we see that it is a prayer. God has made every provision for our spiritual lives, and prayer is the means of obtaining these provisions. So often prayer in the church focuses on physical, tangible needs. While this is not wrong, if we are to grow spiritually and impact the world, we must give as much attention to spiritual needs. Paul understood this, and a study of his prayers reveals some of the things for which we should ask.

1. After we are saved, why should the *knowledge* of God (v. 17) be the most important spiritual goal of our lives?

2. How can you deepen your knowledge of God?

3. In verses 18 and 19 Paul mentioned more things he wanted believers to know. He wanted them to come to a new understanding of these truths because that understanding would change their spiritual lives. How would grasping these three truths change your life?

The *hope* of His calling

The *riches* of the glory of His inheritance

The exceeding greatness of His *power* toward us

4. Why do you think we need to understand that God's power, which works in us, is the same power that raised Christ from death and seated Him in Heaven?

5. What problem or need are you facing right now that requires God's power to work in you?

6. What do you think you must do in order to have God's unhindered power at work in your life?

7. Christ is now seated in His heavenly position of power at God's right hand. He is Lord of His people and His church (composed of all true believers). With verses 20-23 in mind, explain why a believer's drive for power, influence, and fame as a means of personal fulfillment runs contrary to Scripture.

8. What should be our attitude in Christ as we are faced with opportunities for personal advancement? See Philippians 2:2-9.

9. How does our Savior's exalted position assure you that His power is sufficient to meet all your life needs?

10. As a believer, you have the provision of God's power and Christ's position of authority to support you. How can you trust God's power in each of the following areas?

Trying circumstances

Your emotional needs

Material needs and finances

Dealing with problems

Facing the future

Carrying out responsibilities

Struggling with sin

An Illustration to Examine: The Rich Fool

Read Luke 12:16-21. Although the story deals with a man and material goods, let's focus on the man's attitude toward life.

11. Who did the man consult regarding his plans and decisions?

12. What was the man's main focus in life?

13. What should have been his priority?

14. Describe the man's failure.

IV. DROP ANCHOR

In which one of the following areas do you need to make a spiritual decision for change?

___ Jesus Christ *is Lord!* This passage tells us that He has authority over all powers and positions of prestige. He is Lord of His church and each person in it. He is your head. Have you given Christ total control over all areas of your life (thoughts, attitudes, words, behavior, habits, relationships, etc.)? If not, realize that His power cannot be exerted in your life until you yield control to Him. Spend several minutes speaking to Him about this matter. Humbly hand over your life to Him, and commit yourself to allowing Christ to be Lord of your life.

___ The apostle Paul understood the importance of praying deeply spiritual prayers. His requests were centered around qualities that would impact believers' inner lives and their relationship to God. How is your prayer vocabulary? Does it center around material needs, physical problems, mental and emotional burdens? These things do need prayer attention but not to the neglect of our own and others' spiritual needs. Devote time in prayer to the worship of God. Sincerely and openly pray about personal spiritual weaknesses and goals, such as a deeper love for Christ, a clearer understanding of God, a greater zeal for serving Him. Continue to pray about such desires; the Holy Spirit will do the work. Growth will surely come!

___ Are you seeking personal significance by obtaining power? Perhaps through a job, career, or achievement you are seeking to establish your worth in the eyes of those around you. Or, in your local church, are you trying to exert power over others so that you can have control? The Lord might be pointing out another area of your life through which you are trying to boost your self-esteem. God does not want us to despise ourselves, and obtaining credentials is not evil. But our value comes from being created by Him with our unique gifts and abilities, being redeemed from sin's slavery by Christ's death, and being children who are being conformed to the likeness of His Son. All we are is from Him, and any praise must be His. Just as the Lord Jesus had power clothed in humility, God will give us power for living, but the power will be His in us. That will make it pure! Confess to any "grasping" you have been doing as He reveals this to you. Commit yourself to exalt Him in every aspect of your life.

Speak to the Lord about any decisions you have made. Post a verse from the lesson on a 3" x 5" card to remind you of what you have learned this week.

V. STEPPING OUT ON FAITH

The light of God's Word has already significantly directed us toward our desired destination. In the first chapter of Ephesians we have seen that the foundation of personal fulfillment comes in two ways. First of all, we must know God as Father and belong to Him. Secondly, we must grow in the knowledge of Him and see His power at work in our lives to enable us to live effectively for Him.

Admit it or not, we often have a secret dread that God wants to deprive us of all we desire. Actually the Lord wants to give us the desires of our heart (Psalm 37:4), and a satisfying life is one of these. But God's way of attaining a satisfying life and the world's way of finding it are opposed. In fact, the world offers nothing that is totally, permanently satisfying. God doesn't want us to clutch at the world's power for our own pride but to humbly ask for His power with the outstretched hand of prayer. His power can accomplish great things in us, through us, and for us. Now that's fulfillment!

Take Your Place, Please

Ephesians 2

*"For we are his workmanship, created in Christ Jesus
unto good works, which God hath before ordained that
we should walk in them" (Ephesians 2:10).*

Perhaps you can recall an event or a time in your life when you felt very insignificant: being in a huge crowd, being alone, or being at an occasion where someone else was honored. The feelings of isolation that sweep over us at such moments can be frightening. We ask: "Who am I, and who really cares about me? Do I have any importance in this world of swarming humanity?"

Thankfully, Ephesians 2 answers with a resounding YES! The beginning verses do not offer a very pleasant portrayal of who we were before receiving Jesus Christ. But once we are in Him, we find that God has great plans for us. Take heart: He truly cares for you and will work in you so that you can take your place in His great plan. To God, you are a woman of great significance.

I. SOUNDING THE DEPTHS OF YOUR HEART

• Are you presently struggling with a sense of personal insignificance? Why do you think this is?

• If you could be or do anything right now to make yourself feel significant, what would that be?

II. IN LIGHT OF THE SCRIPTURES

Read Ephesians 2.

1. Verses 1-3 paint a picture of the person who has not put her trust in the Lord Jesus Christ and His atoning death on the cross. What description is given of the woman who has not received Christ as her Savior?

2. Hopefully the description above is no longer applicable to you, although at some point in each of our lives, we all lived this way. Read verses 4-16 and list what God did for you at the moment you received His Son into your life. From what attributes of God did you receive these benefits?

3. God did this for us, but not because we deserved it. Verses 1-3 state that we were dead, disobedient, lust-fulfilling sinners. Read verses 7-10; list the reasons God wanted to bring us into a relationship with Himself.

4. Read verses 11-18. Before Christ's first coming, the Ephesians would have been considered spiritual castaways. The Jews alone were God's people, and male circumcision was the outward sign of their special relationship with God. No Gentile (non-Jew) had any hope—except by becoming a Jew. According to verse 13, what does Christ's blood do for us when we look to it as the payment for our sins?

5. In Christ, what is now the status of Jews and Gentiles before God (vv. 14-17)?

6. What privilege is given to all believers in Christ (v. 18)? Explain what you think this means.

7. Paul stated emphatically in verses 19-22 that we now have a place within God's plan. He used three metaphors (illustrations) to describe our position. What are they?

8. As we focus on the building metaphor, draw a diagram of this spiritual structure after you read verses 20-22. Be sure to include yourself.

9. How is this temple described? What is another word for this structure?

10. God is working out His plan, as we have seen in chapter 2. It is a plan for individuals, for Jews and Gentiles, and for the church. We find our significance in life only as we take our appointed place in God's great plan. In summary, state the purposes of God for each group according to the verses listed.

His purpose in saving individual believers—
verse 7

verse 10

His purpose in accepting Gentiles to be His people as well as Jews—
verses 12-14

His purpose in creating His church—
verses 21, 22

III. CHARTING YOUR COURSE

1. Committing sin, following the way of Satan and the world, living to

gratify self—all these actions characterize the one who has not yet received Christ. Yet there are believers in Christ whose lives, even after
many years, still strongly reflect the "old life." As you scan verses 4-9
again, explain why your life in Jesus Christ should be different, a "then"
and "now" scenario. See 2 Corinthians 5:17.

2. One word that is repeated in this passage tells us a necessary ingre-
dient to vanquish the old, dead, sinful life and usher in the new: grace.

(a) What did God's grace do for us (vv. 5, 8)?

(b) What did you do to receive God's grace at the time of your salvation?

(c) What, then, must you do to receive God's grace for living in
Christ daily?

3. In verse 10 the word "workmanship" has the idea of "a work of
art." Paraphrase this verse in a way that applies to you personally. How
does this bring significance to your life?

4. If you are a Gentile (non-Jew), you now can also claim to be one of
"God's people," not by racial birth but by the new birth. In Christ, God
has given you a place near Him (v. 13). Verse 18 states that you have ac-

cess to God through the Spirit. What are some of the spiritual benefits of having access?

5. God has granted us a heavenly citizenship (v. 19). In our daily life on earth, how should this affect the way we live? See Hebrews 11:8-10, 13-16; 1 Peter 2:9-11; 1 John 2:15-17.

6. God has granted us a place in His household. Consider the benefits and privileges that go along with being part of a household. How might this apply to being part of God's household? What might be some of the responsibilities?

7. The establishing of the church of Christ's true believers is compared to the process of building a temple. Each person who places his or her faith in Jesus Christ is another brick added to the structure. What do you learn from this mental picture about your place in Christ's church?

8. Having understood your place of importance within the Body of Christ, the church, how should this carry over to your involvement in your local church?

An Illustration to Examine: The Great Feast

Read Luke 14:15-23.

Jesus told a parable to illustrate God's great mercy in bringing us into a relationship with Himself. Originally, under the Old Covenant, only the Jews were to have access to God. But through Christ's death for us, Gentiles also can share in fellowship with God.

9. How is the behavior of the rude guests (vv. 18-20) an example of the description given in Ephesians 2:2 and 3: "walked according to the course of this world," "children of disobedience," "fulfilling the desires of the flesh and of the mind"?

10. How was the treatment of the poor, maimed, halt, and blind (v. 21) an illustration of Ephesians 2:4-8?

IV. DROP ANCHOR

In which one of the following areas do you need to make a spiritual change?

___ You are a citizen of God's heavenly country, and, as far as He is concerned, you are as good as already there with Christ. Therefore, what you were *before* Christ should no longer characterize your life. Are you following the ways of this world, being disobedient to God's Word? Are you fulfilling your own sinful thoughts and desires? Reflect His mercy, love, and workmanship in your life. Take your place as a heavenly citizen and show forth the riches of His grace.

___ We have seen in this passage that we have significance in this world because God has a position for us to fill and a work for us to accomplish. Are you finding personal significance in life through doing your own work or God's work? Like the busy people of the parable in Luke 14, are you too preoccupied with your own pursuits to fellowship with God? Knowing Him and serving Him should be the focus of your life. Meditate on Ephesians 2:10 and ask God what work He has for you to do. He will show you. As you take your place in God's plan, your need for personal significance will be fulfilled.

___ Have you taken your place in a Bible-teaching local church where Christ is exalted as Savior and Lord? If not, pray about this matter and be open to God's will for you. You need the other "stones" of the spiritual temple for support, and they need you too. God has work for you to do. Take your place in His plan!

Spend a few minutes in prayer with your Heavenly Father, committing any spiritual decisions to Him. Continue to pray about this matter this week. Post a verse to help you with your decision.

V. STEPPING OUT ON FAITH

Can you see that God has a very significant place for YOU? You—who were dead in sin, an object of His wrath, without hope in this life or the one to come—were lovingly chosen by God. You were given spiritual life, a reserved heavenly Home with Christ, access to the Father, citizenship in God's country, a place in God's household, and a position of importance in His holy temple, the church. Where now is that hidden rock of *insignificance?* Fear it no more. Take your place "in Christ." In Him, you are significant indeed!

What Can God Do with Me? Part 1

Ephesians 3

"Unto me, who am less than the least of all saints, is this grace given, that I should preach among the Gentiles the unsearchable riches of Christ" (Ephesians 3:8).

God chose you, adopted you, sealed you, and raised you up to sit in heavenly places with His Son. He created you in Christ to do good works for Him. He made you a citizen of Heaven, a member of His household, and a part of His holy dwelling, the church.

Maybe you're thinking, "Okay; God has done all this for me, but I'm still a person struggling with sin and failure. What, really, can God do *with* me?"

The apostle Paul could have had the same thoughts about himself after becoming a disciple of Christ. He had an infamous past as far as Christians were concerned. And, as he penned this letter to the Ephesians, his circumstances weren't convenient or comfortable for personal ministry.

Let's take a look at Paul's attitude about his own life. As we observe his spiritual focus in Christ, we can be directed to a similar path of spiritual purposefulness.

I. SOUNDING THE DEPTHS OF YOUR HEART

• Is there anything in your life right now that is hindering you from being God's fruitful servant? Fear? inadequacy? pride? self-pity? selfishness? the past? people? circumstances? sin?

• Is this hindrance greater than God's grace toward you? Is it greater than God's power that can work in you?

II. IN LIGHT OF THE SCRIPTURES

Read Ephesians 3.

Paul, years before the writing of this letter, had been a persecutor of Christ's people. Now he was a prisoner in Rome for preaching Christ to others. (You can read his story in Acts 22:1-21.) He had a bad past, but God didn't throw him away as unusable.

1. Verses 2 and 7-9 focus on Paul's calling to be a servant of God. According to verses 2 and 7, what attributes, or qualities, of God enabled Paul to go from being an unprofitable sinner to a fruitful, spiritual servant?

2. Does Paul point to any qualities of his own that enable him to do God's great work?

3. How did Paul refer to himself in verse 8?

4. Do you think Paul felt inadequate to do God's work in his own strength? Did he struggle with self-pity?

5. Referring to verses 3-10, what "mystery" had God revealed to Paul, the apostles, and the prophets (v. 6)?

6. What did Paul consider to be the job God had for him to do (vv. 8, 9)?

7. Believers in Christ Jesus, Jews and Gentiles alike, make up the church, the Body of Christ (v. 6). (a) What does God want to demonstrate through His church (vv. 10, 11)?

(b) Who does He want to observe this?

8. A promise similar to the one given in Ephesians 2:18 is repeated in 3:11 and 12. (a) What is that promise?

(b) On what is it contingent?

9. Paul was in chains in Rome as he wrote this letter to the Ephesian believers. What was His attitude in these negative circumstances as expressed in verse 13?

10. Carefully consider this passage (Ephesians 3:1-13) again. For Paul, what purpose of his life brought personal fulfillment and joy?

III. CHARTING YOUR COURSE

1. Paul had had extensive religious training, Roman citizenship, a prestigious position as a Pharisee, and a zealous, climb-the-success-ladder mentality. Although Paul used his training and citizenship as assets in doing God's work, he totally depended upon God's grace and power to carry out his ministry. How can pride and reliance upon our strengths, accomplishments, and abilities hinder God from working through us?

2. How is doing God's work in our own strength an insult to God?

3. What attitudes are necessary, then, to be usable by God, as Paul was?

4. On the other hand, a self-pitying, falsely humble person is usually not very productive for God either. Why might this be?

5. How is focusing on our own insufficiency an insult to God?

6. What must such a person do to become usable to God?

7. It matters not whether we feel we are gifted or insufficient to do God's work because God does not depend on our strength to carry out His purpose. According to Romans 12:1, what are we to do with our lives and all we are?

8. When Paul wrote to the Ephesians, his circumstances did not seem very favorable for "usability." He was under house arrest in Rome. Yet, God *did* use Paul—even during this time. How? Make a list based on the following references: Acts 28:30, 31; Ephesians 1:16; Philippians 1:12-14; Colossians 4:16.

9. How do we tend to react when circumstances turn against us? Do we usually concentrate on ministering for God when life gets tough?

10. Paul referred to himself as the least of the saints, yet he was used by God to plant Christianity all across the Roman Empire. Paul did not focus on his own personality/abilities/circumstances, but considered himself simply a "channel" through whom God's grace and power could flow out to others. Our weaknesses and sense of inadequacy are actually *good* in that they force us to depend solely upon God to do the work in and through us. Three times in this passage, Paul mentioned God's grace at work in his life. What is grace?

11. What part does grace have in our ministry for God? See 2 Corinthians 12:7-10.

12. As we receive God's grace, He, in turn, will use us to administer grace in others' lives (1 Peter 4:10). Can you relate a time in your life when God's grace enabled you to serve another person and bring glory to Himself?

13. In verse 10 we read that God wants to show His great wisdom through Christ's church to the heavenly powers. Sometimes I wonder, "What can God do with the church?" Because it is composed of imperfect people, it often seems plagued by disagreements, personality clashes, sin, etc. But the church universal (and the local church) is *God's* plan. What can we, the church, demonstrate about God and Christ? Can you think of any verses that address this issue?

14. Verses 11 and 12 remind us that we have access to God in Christ. It is never on our own goodness, sincerity, or devotion that we "earn" the right to come to God or belong to Him. Christ alone is the reason God accepts us and acts on our behalf. This is a necessary stripping away of our own pride. How is this contrary to the way the world tells us to think? Doesn't this tear down our self-esteem? Explain.

An Illustration to Examine: The Vine and Branches
Read John 15:1-11.

15. What does God expect every one of His branches to do? Explain what you think this means.

16. What must we do in order to be fruitful for God?

17. What does Jesus promise as the result of being a fruitful servant of God (v. 11)?

IV. DROP ANCHOR

Evaluate your spiritual service for Christ. Is one of the following areas a hindrance to your working for the Lord?

____ FEAR. Do you find yourself thinking, "I've never done this before/I may fail or make a fool of myself/I'm not adequate to do this"? You must not trust in yourself; trust in God's grace to enable you. Though you may feel like "the least," as Paul did, the great power of God will accomplish His work (2 Timothy 1:7, 8).

____ CIRCUMSTANCES. Perhaps you have a desire to serve God, but your present circumstances have filled you with self-centeredness and self-pity. Commit yourself to God to use you in any way He chooses, despite your situation. He may not use you as you desire or expect, but let Him be in control. Circumstances do not hinder God from using a yielded servant (1 Corinthians 15:57, 58).

____ PRIDE. *I* is always in the middle of pride. Have you been laboring for God but depending on *your* strength, abilities, wisdom, persuasiveness, or cleverness? In truth, you are exalting yourself, not God. Become a Spirit-empowered servant. He will give you grace and power to do God's will God's way. Then, through you, He can exalt His Son and His name (Hebrews 12:28).

____ PEOPLE. Perhaps you have said, "I can't serve—people are just too difficult! Their problems are too complicated, and their personalities are too trying." If we are disciples of Jesus, God wants us to declare to everyone "the unsearchable riches of Christ" (Ephesians 3:8). Perhaps you have been focusing on people as being *nuisances* rather than *needy*. If your heart to serve people has gone cold, ask God to rekindle your compassion and show you the needs He would have you meet (Matthew 28:18-20).

___ SIN. Maybe you're not working for Christ because you're not abiding in Him. What sin are you holding on to? Self-centeredness? past sins and failures? some other disobedience? Let go of it and trust God's power to free you from sin's grip. Seek forgiveness from God and others as needed. Ask Him to make you clean and fruitful. Experience the joy of serving Him (John 15:3, 4, 11).

V. STEPPING OUT ON FAITH

So the question remains, "What can God do with me?" So far, we have this answer: God can do great things with you! But the responsibility rests with you to want to be used of God and to allow His grace to enable you to be used of Him. Whatever hindrances have stood in your way of being useful to God, give them to Him. As He directs you to the work He has planned—yes, created you to do—you will find joy, purpose, and satisfaction. That's fulfillment!

What Can God Do with Me? Part 2

Ephesians 2:19—3:1; 3:14-21

*"Now unto him that is able to do exceeding abundantly
above all that we ask or think, according to the power
that worketh in us" (Ephesians 3:20).*

Our family enjoys watching a certain television show in which
people bring various articles to antiques experts to have them appraised. Almost without exception, the owner of the antique is astonished at the worth of the object. Perhaps it seemed small, plain, or insignificant; the owner supposed it to be of some value, but never so much!
Often the value lies in who made the article. That able artisan endowed
his creation with all the skill, care, and beauty he or she could pour into
it. The item's value rests in the name of its maker and his work as expressed
in that object. Once the appraiser points out its origin and uniqueness,
that plain possession is considered precious and wonderful.

As you look at yourself, maybe you feel plain and insignificant among
the many who are attractive, talented, and accomplished. Dear sister believer, have you come to realize Who it is that created you physically and
then spiritually in Christ Jesus to be a precious and wonderful possession
for Himself? Christ's name is stamped on you, and God is willing to pour
all of His supernatural love, grace, and power into you to make you a
valuable vessel for the Master's work and glory.

In lesson 4 we dealt with the hindrances that keep us from being used
of God. In this lesson, let us focus on the spiritual resources that enable

us to be used of God. He does not expect us to be perfected and productive by our own efforts. We could never do what God wants us to do in our own power.

As we read and study Ephesians 3:14-21, we will see the overflowing promises of all that the Lord will provide: the power to live a daily life of faith and obedience in Christ, the love of God and others that leads to full spiritual maturity. The goal of all this is the glory of Christ and the Father.

God *can* do so much with you as you humbly present yourself to Him—as small and insignificant as you may seem.

I. SOUNDING THE DEPTHS OF YOUR HEART

Evaluate your daily prayer time by answering the following questions.

• Do you pray each day to be filled with the Holy Spirit's power to live a God-pleasing life?

• Do you think about Christ's love for you and ask God to deepen your love for Him and others?

• Do you come before God in prayer with a strong sense of His mighty power that can do great things in you and through you?

II. IN LIGHT OF THE SCRIPTURES

Read Ephesians 2:19—3:1 and 3:14-21.

1. Verse 14 continues Paul's thoughts begun in verse 1, which in turn connects with the topic at the end of chapter 2. (Paul interrupted his train of thought in chapter 2 to divert to verses 2-13 in chapter 3!) Paul returned to the subject of believers in their "churchly" relationships. What are believers *collectively* called in verse 15?

2. What is the special privilege that all believers have, according to verses 14 and 15?

3. What is the goal, expressed in the first part of verse 17, that Paul desired for the life of each of these believers?

4. How is this goal accomplished (v. 16)?

5. After praying for this life of continuing faith, Paul turned his attention to love in verse 17. What do you think it means that we are "rooted and grounded in love"?

6. What did Paul think necessary for his readers to comprehend in verses 18 and 19?

7. What are the "dimensions" of His love?

8. As expressed in verse 19, what will be the result in our lives when we are being strengthened by the Spirit's power (v. 16), having Christ dwell in our hearts daily (v. 17), and being rooted, grounded, and growing in knowledge of His love (v. 19)?

9. What does this mean to you?

10. Paul concluded these thoughts (actually a prayer that began in verse 14) by focusing on our glorious God—the One Who can fill His weak and faltering children with faith, love, and power as He had done in Paul's life. What is God able to do for us according to verse 20?

11. Where will these great things take place?

12. What will accomplish these things?

13. The last verse of Ephesians 3 states what God expects His church to do. What is it?

III. CHARTING YOUR COURSE

1. In lesson 4 we learned that God's grace is a necessary provision if we are to live fulfilling Christian lives. Ephesians 3:17 points out that Christ must *dwell* in our hearts by faith. At the moment we receive Him into our lives as Savior, He does come to dwell in us and will never leave us. But daily we must let His life flow through us. His character will permeate my being as I allow Him to dwell in me by faith. This is a vital truth

for the true believer's life. How is this thought expressed in the following verses?

Galatians 2:20

John 15:5

1 Corinthians 1:30

2. When it comes to love, the issue has two sides: a growing understanding of God's love for you and a growing love in you for God and others. In order for you to be an effective servant, why is it needful for you to grasp the fact that God loves you totally and unconditionally?

3. Through our faith in Christ, we receive God's grace and power to serve. Why must we also be filled with Christ's love to serve God acceptably? See 1 Corinthians 13:1-3 and 1 John 4:11, 12, 19-21.

4. We often quote verse 20 in reference to outward circumstances that we desire God to change. But, in its context, the verse refers to God doing *in us* more than we could ask or think. The goal of verse 19 is full spiritual maturity so that we can love God, live for God, and serve God. Why must we routinely pray for our own spiritual growth and that of others?

5. Based on this passage, what are some of the spiritual requests that you and I need to make daily? Write your answer in the first person to make it personal for you.

6. As individual members of Christ's church, why will we fall short of fully glorifying Christ in this age (v. 21) if we don't pray about inner spiritual qualities?

Illustrations to Examine

7. Let's expand on Ephesians 3:20. How did the people in the following passages limit God in their asking or thinking? Read the passages and explain.

Luke 1:5-20

Matthew 13:53-58

Judges 6:1, 11-16

8. How did the people in the following passages express their trust in God's power to do great things through them or for them?
1 Samuel 17:4, 32-37, 45, 46

Matthew 8:5-13

9. What are some of the attitudes in our lives that may cause us to limit God's work? Give specific examples of how we as believers limit God in our thinking or asking. Maybe you have a personal illustration.

IV. DROP ANCHOR

Perhaps the Lord has convicted you of a need in one of the following areas. Commit your need to Him in prayer this week.

___ I need to abide in Christ daily by faith, so that He can dwell in and live through me. I am asking God to help me grow in this faith relationship so that I can live an abundant Christian life.

___ I need to rest more fully in Christ's love for me. I am asking the Lord to help me grow in this knowledge and asking that my love for Him and others will increase as I understand His great love for me.

___ I desire a greater spiritual maturity. I am asking God to show me the areas of my life in which I am hindering or limiting Him. I want to pray for spiritual growth every day.

V. STEPPING OUT ON FAITH

Even as a believer in Christ, perhaps you have never really allowed God to change your life by letting His grace and power have total freedom to do their transforming work. God can take you, His frail little child, and by His Spirit fill you with strength and ability to do His will. Each day, come to Christ by faith. As you let Him dwell in your heart and have control, He will do God's work in and through you. As soon as you slip from that "faith position" and take control of your life and abilities, you are not totally dependent on God; you will squelch the working of His power. The end results are unfruitful or, at best, temporary. God's goal for us is "spiritual fullness." It comes through Him Who is able to do more than we mere created beings can imagine. And our spiritual fullness brings glory to Him, now and throughout all eternity. That's what He can do with us!

Come Aboard!

Ephesians 4:1-16

"Till we all come in the unity of the faith, and of the knowledge of the Son of God, unto a perfect man, unto the measure of the stature of the fulness of Christ" *(Ephesians 4:13).*

As we sail toward God's land of fulfillment, it is pleasant to find that we are not alone. It's not just me in my little sailboat! Christ, the Captain of our salvation, calls us aboard to join His other crew members. He will teach us all, together, as we journey along. And there's so much for us to learn!

One of the first things we need to understand as believers is the difference between "position" and "practice." Knowing your position in Christ (what God declares to be true of you now that you are His) is vital and must precede your practice in Christ (how you actually live in this world now that you are His). For example, God declares in His Word that you *are* holy (1 Peter 2:9), yet in your thoughts, attitudes, words, and actions you may see much that is unholy. In practice, you must move continually closer to your position of holiness.

As we have seen, God has made every supernatural provision for this process to take place: His grace, His power, the privilege of prayer, even the very presence of Christ in us to live out His life through us. Our responsibility, always, is to respond to His work and obey His Word.

As we begin Ephesians 4, we will find further provision for our growth in spiritual maturity: the true church. Here, in very practical and tangible form, the Lord has given us another source of help and encouragement. Don't go it alone; come aboard!

I. SOUNDING THE DEPTHS OF YOUR HEART

Circle your answer for each of the following evaluation questions.

Do you belong to a Christ-exalting, Bible-teaching church?	No	Yes
Do you regularly attend all services?	No	Yes
Do you think you are growing in your understanding of the basic doctrines and principles of the Christian life?	No	Yes
Are you actively involved in some church ministry?	No	Yes
Do you think you are using the spiritual gift God has given you?	No	Yes

II. IN LIGHT OF THE SCRIPTURES

Read Ephesians 4:1-16.

Paul always worked from the positional to the practical, from the doctrinal to the "do." After reviewing in Ephesians 1—3 our doctrinal beliefs and position in Christ, he turned his attention to our practice. Paul told his readers that because of all these supernatural mercies, they are to live a life worthy of their calling in Christ; they are not to be spiritual failures. In a very down-to-earth way, the readers are about to be instructed how to be "heavenly" in the particulars of life.

1. According to verse 1, what are we expected to do as Christians?

2. What qualities are mentioned in verses 2 and 3 that are to characterize our conduct toward other believers?

3. What is the goal of this conduct (v. 3)?

4. Who accomplishes unity in the church (v. 3)?

5. Look closely at verses 1-3 again. How do you understand "unity" to be accomplished in a local church according to these verses?

6. What is the point of Paul's listing all of these "ones" in verses 4-6? How do these "ones" promote unity?

7. Today's world tells us to look out for No. 1 (ourselves). As Paul continued his letter, he stressed God's plan for believers to be in a local church where they will care for others and be cared for in return. According to verses 7-10, what two things has Christ given us in the wake of His ascension and enthronement in Heaven?

8. Every believer has received a spiritual gift from Christ—not for her own good, but for the good of the church. (See Romans 12:4-8; 1 Corinthians 12:4-7; 1 Peter 4:10.) In verse 11, certain "callings" are listed. What are these? Use a Bible dictionary to define each of these ministries.

9. According to verse 12, what is the role of these leaders within the church?

10. What is the Lord's primary purpose for putting His children into this dynamic group, the church (vv. 13, 14)?

11. What essential part of the Christian growth process is mentioned in verse 15?

12. Verses 15 and 16 seem to contradict each other. Christ is the One Who causes His church to grow, yet who is doing the work? Can you explain how Christ is doing the work?

III. CHARTING YOUR COURSE

1. You can never "pay" God for your eternal life, but God does expect you to live a life that is worthy of that gift. What kind of life do you think that is? Read Colossians 3:1-4, Galatians 5:16-25, 1 Peter 2:9-12, and Romans 12:1-3.

2. God has designed the church to assist us in living this worthy life. The church is a training camp where we learn to conduct ourselves in a godly way. How can we exhibit the qualities in verse 2 toward people who are stubborn, demanding, rude, etc.?

3. "Unity" is a word that is thrown about in Christian circles but not always clearly understood from a Biblical perspective. What might be some of the things people call "unity" that are not in line with God's Word?

4. A. W. Tozer described unity with this illustration: a hundred pianos, all tuned to the same tuning fork, will be in tune with each other. What did he mean by this? What verses in our passage reflect this idea?

5. Are you growing in your understanding of true Bible doctrine? This is essential for your spiritual stability (v. 14). What are some of the ways you are deepening your understanding of Scripture, especially fundamental doctrines?

6. We were told in verse 15 that "speaking the truth in love" is a needful part of each Christian's growth. Sometimes the pastor, a Bible teacher, or fellow believer may need to speak so to us, or perhaps the Lord may burden us to speak so to another Christian. Consider and answer each of the following questions.

   (a) What is "truth"?

   (b) How do we speak "in love"?

   (c) Why is this necessary for growing in Christ?

   (d) How does God demonstrate this concept toward us?

   (e) Some people speak the truth without love. How can this be detrimental to a person's spiritual growth?

(f) Some people emphasize only love. How can this be a hindrance to spiritual growth?

(g) What should be our response when someone speaks the truth in love to us?

7. Pastor-teachers are to equip the *people* of the church to serve and build up one another. Tell what each of these phrases means to you in relation to your responsibility to your church.

"Endeavouring to keep the unity of the Spirit" (v. 3)

"Grow up into him [Christ] in all things" (v. 15)

"The effectual working . . . of every part" (v. 16)

An Illustration to Examine: Priscilla, Aquila, Apollos
Read Acts 18:24-28.
8. How did Aquila and Priscilla minister to Apollos?

9. How did Apollos minister to believers?

10. Think for a moment how different this beautiful scenario could have been if each party had reacted without meekness and concern for the unity of faith and the work of God! Discuss the possibilities.

11. Christ, your Captain, has called you to come on board. Explain how being part of a local church has helped you personally to advance toward Christian maturity and stability.

IV. DROP ANCHOR

Select one of the following areas in which the Lord has shown you the need for a change.

___ I need to "walk worthy" of my position in Christ.

___ I need Christ's lowliness, meekness, longsuffering, forbearance, and love to characterize my relationship with others.

___ I need a deeper knowledge and understanding of the fundamental doctrines of the faith.

___ I need to do my part in the church to build up other Christians.

___ I need to respond with openness when others speak the truth of God to me in love.

___ I need to be sensitive to the Holy Spirit and be bold enough to speak the truth in love to others as He directs me.

Commit this need to God in prayer and continue to pray about it this week. In what practical way can you seek to obey God in this area? What verse in this passage can you post to meditate on this week?

V. STEPPING OUT ON FAITH

On our journey we will often be buffeted by the strong winds of Satan's lies and deceit. He will try anything to get us off course. If we were each alone in our own little craft, how quickly we would capsize!

But aboard our Savior's ship, we work together as a crew. As Christians we must be careful that in our quest for fulfillment, we don't become selfish and self-centered. God never intended us to find fulfillment by that route. Rather, a great deal of our satisfaction will come by serving others, just as Christ did. We have our work orders. Our Captain has given us leaders to train us and "show us the ropes." We, in turn, are to strengthen the hands of our fellow crew members and work alongside them.

What a wonderful plan is God's church! There is strength in numbers. As we pull together around common doctrine and common goals, we will see the fruit of true unity, produced by the Spirit, in which each of us is needed and each need is met.

Leave That Old Life Behind

Ephesians 4:17-32

"That ye put off concerning the former conversation the old man, which is corrupt according to the deceitful lusts; And be renewed in the spirit of your mind; And that ye put on the new man, which after God is created in righteousness and true holiness" (Ephesians 4:22-24).

We have learned that God totally accepts us if we are "in Christ." He has provided great resources to make us glorifying, fruitful servants of God. As His children, we are to grow up and conduct ourselves as citizens of His heavenly realm.

Unlike many immigrants who come to a new land bringing their old habits, customs, and lifestyle, we must develop a totally new life when we receive Christ. Second Corinthians 5:17 states, "Therefore if any man be in Christ, he is a new creature: old things are passed away; behold, all things are become new." God's Spirit works to eliminate from our daily lives all that characterized us before we belonged to Christ. Our part is to yield to His work and obey as He directs us by God's Word. Yes, the standards of this new life are high, but again, God Himself has provided the power to live such a life.

So, journeying onward, we leave that old life farther behind, and desiring to be fulfilled women of God, we press on toward the new life He desires us to live.

I. SOUNDING THE DEPTHS OF YOUR HEART

Is your life marred by any of these "old life" characteristics?

___ ignorance of God's Word, resulting in spiritual instability and sinful living

___ moral impurity in thought or behavior

___ greed, deceitful desires (things that appear to bring happiness, but don't)

___ lying

___ sinful anger, fits of rage, malice, arguing

___ stealing

___ unwholesome speech (slander, gossip, criticizing, etc.)

___ bitterness, rage, fighting, malice

II. IN LIGHT OF THE SCRIPTURES

Read Ephesians 4:17-32.

1. In verses 17-24 Paul contrasted the "old life" with the "new life." He started out strongly in verse 17 by telling the Ephesians they *must not* behave as unbelievers do. Describe the mind of an unregenerate person and explain what each word or phrase means (vv. 17, 18).

2. Describe the heart of an unbeliever (v. 18).

3. Describe the behavior, in general, of those outside Christ (v. 19).

4. According to verses 20 and 21, what causes a Christian to be different?

5. What three things are we commanded to do in verses 22-24?

6. (a) What qualities will diminish (v. 22)?

(b) What qualities will increase (v. 24)?

7. Beginning at verse 25, Paul listed certain "old life" behaviors and the "new life" alternative. What is the behavior named in verse 25 that is no longer to be part of a Christian's life?

8. What is the commanded alternative? What reason is given in this verse?

9. Verse 26 deals with anger. What should be our response when we are overcome by feelings of anger?

10. What other two directives are given in verses 26 and 27 about handling our anger? Explain what these two commands mean.

11. What remedy for stealing did Paul put forth in verse 28?

12. Corrupt communication is sinful speech that belongs to the old life. With what kind of speech are we to replace it (v. 29)?

13. By way of summary, Paul commanded his readers not to grieve the Holy Spirit (v. 30). He is the One Who enables us to live this new godly life, and we grieve Him when we do that which is contrary to God's will. List all the "old life" sins that are not to be a part of your life now, as mentioned in verse 31.

14. What "new life" qualities, similar to those that were listed at the beginning of chapter 4, are commanded in verse 32?

15. What is the supreme reason for our merciful and gracious behavior toward others?

III. CHARTING YOUR COURSE

1. Our lives are determined in great part by what is going on in our minds. Our dead spirits, at the moment of our salvation, were immediately made alive by God (Ephesians 2:1-5), but the renewal of our minds is a process that takes some time. Because our thoughts lead directly to attitudes, words, and actions, they must be closely controlled and guarded. What "old life" habits and influences must you avoid in order to put off the vanity, darkness, and blindness of the world's way of thinking?

2. In what way does the world promote the following sins as being desirable? In contrast, what does God say?

Lasciviousness

Greed

Deceitful lusts

3. How can we pursue the renewing of our minds?

4. How can we pursue righteousness and true holiness?

5. List every kind of lying you can think of. Why should a Christian always speak the truth?

6. When we become angry, our tendency is to think about the offense over and over and to embellish our anger by additional thoughts. Describe how to deal with anger in a way that will avoid giving Satan a foothold. Here are some verses to consider: Matthew 18:15; Philippians 4:8; Hebrews 4:15, 16; James 4:6-8; 1 Peter 2:21-23.

7. List different ways that people can steal. How do Christians sometimes justify stealing?

8. On a more positive note, in what ways can our speech be edifying and minister grace?

9. God expects us to live at peace with all people as much as possible (Romans 12:18). This is not always easy, but as we put on the "new life" of the Lord Jesus and focus on working together as fellow crew members, conflict should be minimized. Has a "wall" developed between you and another believer? Has anger or wrath developed into bitterness or malice (wishing ill on a person)? Do you find yourself speaking evil of that person? How can you apply verse 32 to your relationship with that one? What steps would God have you take to get along with this person?

An Illustration to Examine: Zacchaeus
Read Luke 19:1-10.

10. Zacchaeus was a tax collector who got rich collecting extra for himself. How do we know that Zacchaeus received a new life from the Lord Jesus?

11. How did Zacchaeus show his commitment to Christ?

12. What "old life" behaviors did he leave behind?

IV. DROP ANCHOR

Examine Section I again. What "old life" behavior or attitude are you struggling with at present? Which verse(s) in our passage would address this problem?

Pray throughout this week about this spiritual need. Meditate on the verse(s). What specific actions might help you in this problem?

V. STEPPING OUT ON FAITH

The land we're leaving behind (Satan's domain) is a land of bondage. In our blindness, we often don't see that so many of the "old life" behaviors and attitudes keep us chained up and dragged down.

But we can be free! Sin no longer has the right to rule over us (Romans 6). We have left that old land and now have a new life in our Savior, a life that is like His. Leave the old life customs, habits, and lifestyle behind. Christ's life for us is so much more desirable, so much more fulfilling. May we set our sights on drawing ever closer to it.

Light Living

Ephesians 5:1-21

"For ye were sometimes darkness, but now are ye light in the Lord: walk as children of light" (Ephesians 5:8).

In the hymn "Let the Lower Lights Be Burning," Philip P. Bliss referred to "the lights along the shore." I recall reading that a maritime disaster occurred in Bliss's day due to a certain person's failure to light the lower lights along the shore. Evidently Bliss was distressed about the loss of a life due to neglect and penned this hymn, relating the incident to the spiritual realm.

"God is light," the Bible declares. In this study we've likened His Word to a lighthouse that unfailingly guides us on life's voyage. We also are to be "little lights," reflecting God's own character and His Word to those lost in the darkness. If we neglect our relationship to Christ or willfully let our light be snuffed out by the darkness of sinful living, we are not fulfilled Christians. We fail to be what He wants us to be and fail to do what He wants us to do in a world staggering in spiritual darkness. God has called us to "light living," as we see in Ephesians 5:1-21.

I. SOUNDING THE DEPTHS OF YOUR HEART

Evaluate your daily life—thoughts, attitudes, words, and actions. Can you see development of these "new life" qualities taking place in you?

___ following God

___ acting in love, as Christ did

___ offering your total self to God daily

___ living "cleanly," as a saint should

___ avoiding the dark, sinful influences of the world

___ living carefully, using time wisely, doing God's will

___ being filled with the Spirit, having joy and thankfulness in your heart

___ having harmonious relationships with others

II. IN LIGHT OF THE SCRIPTURES

Read Ephesians 5:1-21.

1. In chapter 5 Paul continued to urge the Ephesian believers to live in the new life Christ had provided for them. What command is given in verse 1? What is the reason cited?

2. What is the command in verse 2? What reason is cited this time?

3. What did Christ's love for the Father motivate Him to do (v. 2)? How can we do the same? See Romans 6:11-13; 12:1; 2 Corinthians 5:14, 15.

4. God calls us saints when we become His children (v. 3). What does the word "saint" mean? (Review question 1 in lesson 1.)

5. What kinds of behavior, according to verses 3-5, are inappropriate for saints? List them and define.

6. In verses 6 and 7, what dangers were lurking for the believers as related to these sins just mentioned? What did Paul command believers in verse 7?

7. "Light and dark" is an often-used symbolism in Scripture for the contrast between God's holiness and sin. Paul used this metaphor to show believers how to live. As Christians, how do we get our "light" (v. 8)?

8. How can we walk as children of the light (vv. 9, 10)?

9. Rather than indulge in the works of darkness, what are we to do (v. 11)? What does this mean?

10. Verses 12 and 13 talk about sin, shame, and secret. One indication that we are sinning is that we don't want people, especially other Christians, to know what we are doing, saying, or thinking. Darkness and hiding often accompany sin (Genesis 3:8-12; John 3:19, 20). What reminder about secret sin did Paul give in these verses?

11. To what is the sinner compared in verse 14?

12. In sharp contrast to those who walk in sin's darkness are the children of light. Paul laid out the lifestyle of light in verses 15-21. What does it mean to "walk circumspectly" (v. 15)? What quality is this said to enhance in our lives?

13. What does "redeeming the time" mean? Why are we to do this (v. 16)?

14. What will assure us that we will live carefully and make good use of our time (v. 17)?

15. The children of darkness are often controlled by worldly desires and habits, such as drugs, alcohol, greed (yet they think they are free!). By Whom are we to be controlled (v. 18)?

16. For the children of light, one of the outward expressions of being filled with the Spirit is the expression of worship and joy through godly music. (a) What three types of music are mentioned in verse 19?

(b) Where does the worship take place?

(c) To whom is it directed?

17. Another expression of Spirit-filled living is mentioned in verse 20. What is it?

18. Spirit-filled living also affects our relationships. How (v. 21)?

19. Read 1 John 1:7. What does walking in the light enable us to have with other believers?

III. CHARTING YOUR COURSE

1. Perhaps as a Christian, your life up to this point has been one of straying on and off God's desired course for you. It might be that you need to fully surrender yourself to God's control. Yes, you have received His gift of salvation through faith in His Son, but now you must make a *choice* to give your life totally over to Him if you have never done so. The following phrases from our passage remind us that God expects no halfway

commitment to Christ. Explain what these phrases teach you about your relationship to Him.

(a) "Be ye . . . followers of God" (v. 1)

(b) "A sacrifice to God" (v. 2)

(c) "As becometh saints" (v. 3)

2. Many Christians today are confused or ignorant about what things please or dishonor the Lord. Yet God commands us to know. Explain how the following phrases, if obeyed, will keep you living in the light.

(a) "Walk in love, as Christ also hath loved us" (v. 2)

(b) "Let no man deceive you with vain words" (v. 6)

(c) "Proving [testing] what is acceptable unto the Lord" (v. 10)

(d) "Understanding what the will of the Lord is" (v. 17)

(e) "Be filled with the Spirit" (v. 18; see also verse 9)

3. What are some ways you, as a believer, can live carefully?

4. If we are seeking fulfilled lives, how can we use our time wisely from God's point of view? List any verses you know that instruct us about this matter.

5. "Be filled with the Spirit" is a command. A more accurate translation of the Greek is, "Keep on being filled with the Spirit." How is a believer filled with the Spirit?

Illustrations to Examine

Read each of the following passages and jot down how it illustrates the need for "light living" as taught in Ephesians 5:1-21.

6. Acts 8:9-24. What sins of darkness did Simon the sorcerer need to put off if he were a true believer?

7. In the Acts passage above, how did Peter demonstrate "light living"?

8. Acts 19:17-20. How did these new believers show that they wanted to be children of light?

IV. DROP ANCHOR

Has the Lord spoken to you about any one of the following areas? If so, spend some time in prayer, committing your need to Him and determining what you must do to obey Him.

   ___ I need to surrender my life totally to the Lord and seek to be a saint, by His power, in every area of life.

   ___ I have some "secret" sins that are hidden from others. I want to walk in the light and give up anything that hinders me from being open with God and others.

   ___ I haven't been living carefully or discerning the time. I know God has work for me to do. I want to refine these areas of my life so I can live in God's will daily:_____.

   ___ I have never really understood what it means to be filled with the Spirit. Every day I want to confess all known sin, ask God for the filling of His Spirit, believe He is filling me, and yield and obey as He leads.

V. STEPPING OUT ON FAITH

Being a follower of God, a saint, has benefits. Walking in love and light brings fulfillment. How so? Getting rid of sin and evil from our lives helps eliminate many problems. Of course, some problems we face are not due to personal sin and are beyond our control. But many people are burdened and anxious because of their own doing: immorality, greed, careless living, and unthankful attitudes.

As children of light, we will find that many of life's rough waves are made smooth just by doing God's will. That's a benefit! Love, joy, purity, fruitfulness, thankfulness—Christ truly wants the very best for us!

Right Responses to Our Roles

Ephesians 5:21—6:9

"Knowing that whatsoever good thing any man doeth, the same shall he receive of the Lord, whether he be bond or free" (Ephesians 6:8).

Every woman has many different relationships and roles in life. She may be a wife, mother, employee, or employer. She may be a child of living parents. She is a citizen of a country and perhaps the member of a church assembly.

Every part of a Christian woman's life is affected by her belonging to Jesus Christ. And, if she is to find fulfillment in life, her roles and relationships must be in accord with God's Word.

Attitudes have much to do with our relationships to various people. Sometimes our wrong attitudes cause us to react rather than respond in God's way. We cannot change people—only God can do that. But we can be sure that we respond as children of light.

In this very practical portion of Ephesians, Paul tackled some of our people-related perplexities. When we're drowning in difficulties, godly attitudes can be the lifeline that pulls us back to a right response in our relationships. The Holy Spirit is ready to enable us. Are we ready to obey?

I. SOUNDING THE DEPTHS OF YOUR HEART

On a scale of 1 to 10 (1 being terrible, 10 being perfect), rate yourself in your roles.

___ As a wife, how would you rate the harmony of your relationship with your husband?

___ As a child of your parents, how would you rate your honor of your mother/father?

___ As an employee, how would you rate your overall daily work attitude?

___ As an employer, how would you rate your treatment of your employees?

II. IN LIGHT OF THE SCRIPTURES

Read Ephesians 5:21—6:9.

1. Let's review the final verse of our last lesson, for this is in many ways a preparatory thought to this lesson. (a) As stated in Ephesians 5:21, what should be our general attitude toward other believers?

(b) Who enables us to have this attitude? (v. 18)?

2. (a) What is the motive for this attitude (v. 21)?

(b) Why is this a motive?

3. The idea expressed in Ephesians 5:21 is similar to that of Philippians 2:2-4 (part of the great "submission" passage). How is submission described there?

4. Biblically, what does it mean to submit ourselves to another?

5. To whom is a wife to be in submission, according to verse 22?

6. What is the reason for her submission (v. 23)?

7. What model did Paul use as an illustration of the wife's relationship to her husband?

8. In verses 25-30 Paul instructed husbands how to truly minister to their wives' needs, again using Christ as the model. List the verbs (action words) that command or imply what husbands are to do.

9. According to verse 31, what is the Biblical mindset of a man and woman to be after they are married?

10. What is the proper relationship with parents after the marriage union takes place?

11. What godly attitude must a wife maintain toward her husband (v. 33)? Look up and define this word.

12. Verses 1-4 of chapter 6 focus on the relationships of parents and children. What two commands are given to children regarding parents?

13. What promise, quoted from Exodus 20:12, did God give to the Israelites concerning honor and obedience to parents (v. 3)? What might adding a promise to the commandment show?

14. A special directive is given to fathers in verse 4. What *shouldn't* they do? What *should* they do?

15. In the days of the Roman Empire when Paul lived, many people were slaves. Many slaves became disciples of Christ upon hearing the gospel, and Paul had instruction for them. Although in our Western culture slavery no longer exists, the employee-employer relationship has points of similarity since both deal with working for someone. What attitudes ought a worker to maintain toward the one who is over her? List these attitudes from verses 5-7.

16. What is the spiritual basis for doing good work according to verses 6-8?

17. What instruction is given to masters in their dealings with those under their authority (v. 9)?

III. CHARTING YOUR COURSE

1. We live in a culture that views submission of any sort as being weak and self-deflating. As children of God, who are not of this world, we need to be sure we have proper, Biblical guidelines for our conduct. Submission means not fighting to come out on top, but yielding ourselves to

others and God, Who will exalt us in due time. What attitudes in us hinder our willingness to submit? (Consider 1 Peter 5:6 and 7.)

2. Husbands have the very difficult task of loving their wives as Christ loves the church! As women, it is easy for us to detect all the ways in which husbands fail. How can a wife encourage her husband to do each of the following:

love his wife?

give of himself for his wife?

sanctify his wife?

nourish his wife?

cherish his wife?

3. A wife is to reverence her husband. This means she is to truly honor and respect him as her head. What are some very practical ways she can do this—

in her thoughts and attitudes?

in her words?

in her actions?

4. What if a woman has a husband whom she feels is not worthy of respect? How can she properly carry out her role?

5. You are no longer a child, but perhaps your parents are still living. How can you continue to show them godly honor even as an adult?

6. (a) In the workplace employees often focus on collecting the paycheck. This is far from the attitude our Lord desires from us. God expects us to glorify Him in every task, big or small. Read Ephesians 6:5-8 again, noting

godly attitudes. Write a description of what your daily mind-set should be as you do your work.

(b) How will this mindset help you find fulfillment?

(c) How will it help you deal with an unreasonable employer?

Illustrations to Examine: Godly Role Models

Select at least one of the following passages and answer the questions.

7. *Genesis 13:7-18.* (a) How did Abram show submission to Lot in this situation?

(b) How did God exalt Abram?

(c) How did Abram display the "fear of God"?

8. *1 Samuel 1:1-10, 19-23.* (a) How did Hannah show reverence toward her husband? (Consider especially how she did NOT treat him.)

    (b) Though submissive, how did Hannah show strength of character?

    (c) Point out evidences that Hannah's attitudes encouraged her husband's loving, giving, nourishing, and cherishing.

9. *John 19:25-27.* How did Jesus show deep respect and honor for His mother?

10. *Genesis 24:1-27, 50, 51.* We learned in Ephesians 6 that a worker is to obey (because of accountability), to serve willingly and cheerfully, and to do his or her work for the Lord. How did Abraham's servant demonstrate these qualities?

11. *Ruth 2:4.* How does this one short verse attest to the fact that Boaz was a godly employer?

IV. DROP ANCHOR

In what area has God's Word instructed you through the lesson? Jot down the changes God would have you make with His grace.

_____ In submitting to other people

_____ In my relationship to my husband

_____ In relation to my parents

_____ Toward my employer

_____ Toward my employees

Spend some time in prayer, asking God to work His will in this relationship. Post a verse from the lesson to keep this need in your heart and prayers throughout the week.

V. STEPPING OUT ON FAITH

It often seems that the greatest conflicts and challenges we face in life arise out of our relationships with people. God knows this and has given us an abundance of "relationship guidelines" in His Word. The woman who rightly responds to people through God's enabling will find herself to be a source of blessing and encouragement to others. This is just another means of finding fulfillment and bringing praise to His glory (Ephesians 1:12).

What the Successful Woman Really Wears

Ephesians 6:10-24

"Finally, my brethren, be strong in the Lord, and in the power of his might. Put on the whole armour of God, that ye may be able to stand against the wiles of the devil" *(Ephesians 6:10, 11).*

The phrase "dress for success" was popular several years ago. It seemed that the "experts" (whoever they are) determined that, in the business world, wearing particular apparel would contribute to one's poise and confidence, and ultimately, one's success.

The Lord is also concerned about believers' dressing for success—spiritual success, that is. But the wardrobe He suggests for us is to be warrior's wear. And what's more, this apparel is invisible!

In the journey to fulfillment, we will have battles to fight. Satan wants to hinder us from finding God's fair land. If our powerful enemy can't cause us to steer into the rocks of insignificance, rejection, and failure, if he can't blow us off course through the winds of false doctrine, he will launch an all-out attack upon us by his hoard of demons.

If this sounds like a fairy tale, be assured it isn't. The Bible attests to the fact that the Devil and his legions are real. But the Captain of our salvation, the Lord Jesus Christ, has already defeated Satan at the cross and will one day cast him into the Lake of Fire (Revelation 20:10).

Until then, we must depend upon our Lord's power and arm ourselves for spiritual victory. This armor, when worn daily, will assure us of success in the daily conflicts of life. What are you wearing today?

I. SOUNDING THE DEPTHS OF YOUR HEART

I trust that as you have worked through this study on Ephesians, you have been examining your heart and life. Perhaps you view your life as fulfilling because you have received Christ as Savior and are allowing God to change and guide you. Or possibly you see your life as unfulfilling and failing because Satan has managed to get you off God's course for you. Which statement best sums up your life at this point?

___ My life is fulfilling because I am on God's course for me.

___ I am allowing God to make changes in my life, and I am now heading toward fulfillment.

___ My life has been unfulfilling, and I need God's help to get on course.

II. IN LIGHT OF THE SCRIPTURES

Read Ephesians 6:10-24.

1. In his final words to the Ephesian believers, Paul alerted them to the reality of spiritual (unseen, but evident!) conflict. Remember, this is the practical portion of his letter. This conflict is real and played out in everyday life! Paul began at the climax. What two acts will assure us of winning the daily conflict (vv. 10, 11)?

2. Against whom is the fight? How are these enemies described (vv. 11, 12)? Look up any unfamiliar words in this passage.

3. Whom do these spiritual enemies attack?

4. What does God expect us to be able to do in the battle (vv. 13, 14)?

5. Describe the first action we are to take as mentioned in verse 14.

6. With what do we do this?

7. Why would we "gird our loins" with truth as the first step in preparing for spiritual battles?

8. What other piece of armor does verse 14 direct us to put on? What areas does this piece protect?

9. How can righteousness protect us from Satan? See Revelation 12:10; Romans 3:20-26; 1 Corinthians 1:30; Proverbs 11:6.

10. A soldier in battle needs firm footing so that he won't slip and fall. According to verse 15, what prepares us to stand in the midst of battle?

11. What is the "gospel"? See 1 Corinthians 15:1-4.

12. How does the gospel give us peace in the battle?

13. What is the next piece of equipment, mentioned in verse 16? What is it for?

14. What protects our heads, or minds (v. 17)?

15. How does salvation protect our minds? See Romans 12:2; Ephesians 4:22-24; Philippians 4:6-8.

16. What are our two weapons against evil (vv. 17, 18)?

17. Some argue that a sword is a defensive weapon; some say an offensive weapon. Spiritually speaking, how can the Word of God be both of these for us?

18. Jot down the things verse 18 teaches about prayer.

19. In the midst of spiritual battle, Paul never focused on himself. What was his desire at all times (vv. 19, 20)?

20. A fulfilled woman will experience the beautiful qualities for which the discontented people of the world long. What are three of these (v. 23), and how are they obtained (v. 24)?

III. CHARTING YOUR COURSE

1. Believers have a secure place in Heaven, so what is Satan's desire in attacking them?

2. We are to know Satan's schemes, and one of his schemes is to twist our understanding of God's character. What are some of the lies Satan throws at us about God that can cause us to lose the conflict?

3. The book of Ephesians instructs us to be totally dependent on God's power for every spiritual need. What are some of the erroneous thoughts we may have about ourselves that may keep us from depending on God?

4. This apparel for the well-dressed, fulfilled woman is spiritual and invisible, but it must be worn daily if we are to withstand Satan. How can we put on our armor each day?

5. We must be solidly grounded in truth. Our spiritual well-being de-

pends upon it. List the ways you are learning God's Word. How can you be sure you are not being led into error?

An Illustration to Examine: Tychicus

Read Ephesians 6:21 and 22.

6. Paul's letters introduce us to a vast array of little-known people who were Paul's support system as he ministered in every corner of the Roman Empire. Based on these two verses, explain how Tychicus possessed the three qualities mentioned in verse 23.

Peace

Love

Faith

7. As a daughter of God, do you see the growth of peace, love, and faith (faithfulness) in your life? Do you see yourself as being on course to God's land of fulfillment?

IV. DROP ANCHOR

What changes would the Lord have you make in your life as a result of this study?

___ I need to be more aware of the spiritual conflict that may account for trials I encounter.

___ I need to "dress" each morning by putting on my armor through Bible reading, meditation, and prayer.

___ I need to pray for specific opportunities to share the gospel of Christ boldly.

___ I need to pray diligently about my growth in faith, peace, and love as I press toward God's life of fulfillment for me.

V. STEPPING OUT ON FAITH

As we draw nearer to the blessed shores of fulfillment, we're sure to find that our ship and crew are being pursued by that old enemy, Satan. How assuring to know that our Captain, Jesus Christ, is with us and has provided an invincible armor for each of us to wear.

Much of this armor is "forged" by God's Word: the girdle of truth (all truth rests on God's Word), the breastplate of righteousness (the acquisition of righteousness is defined by Scripture), the peace of the gospel (taught to us in the Word), the helmet of salvation (known through God's revelation of His plan), the shield of faith (strengthened as we absorb Scripture), and finally the Sword of the Spirit, which is the Word of God itself. Even the weapon of prayer, to be effective, should be saturated with Scripture.

Does this leave any doubt that you and I must, above all things, be students of God's Word? If we neglect it, we leave ourselves vulnerable to attack and spiritual injury.

Dress for success, my friend! Each morning, by the reading, study, and application of God's truth, put on the whole armor of God. Fulfillment isn't in fashions, but in standing victorious in Christ in the spiritual battles of this life.

Conclusion

Every woman longs for a fulfilling life. The world boasts about showing us the right route to personal success; but in truth, only God, Who made us and knows us, can direct our course to contentment and productivity.

Though we are all sinners, as the Bible emphatically declares (Romans 3:23), God has not cast us aside as being worthless and useless. His unconditional love for us moved Him to develop a plan for our redemption and fulfillment as human beings. He sent His only Son, Jesus Christ, to live on this earth and die on a cross for the punishment of our sins. Christ rose from death and ascended into Heaven from where He waits to return for those who have received Him into their lives as Savior.

Receiving Christ is the first step toward finding full satisfaction in life. Having made that choice, a woman can then go on to gain a rich life of acceptance, spiritual accomplishment, and victory. The journey is not easy; God never promised it would be. But He has promised His power, grace, love, and light to accompany us all the way. He "is able to do exceeding abundantly above all that we ask or think, according to the power that worketh in us" (Ephesians 3:20).

Are you sailing in the light of the Scriptures? Are you charting the course of your life according to God's will? Are you ready to drop anchor and step out in faith on the shores of godly fulfillment? The Lord Jesus, your Captain, is with you all the way. His promises are sure, and His power is sufficient as you abide in Him by faith. Your fulfillment is for His glory!

LEADER'S
GUIDE

SUGGESTIONS FOR LEADERS

The Bible is a living and powerful book! It is God speaking to us today. Every opportunity to learn from it is a precious privilege. As you use this study guide, be flexible. It is simply a tool to aid in the understanding of God's Word. Adapt it to suit your unique group of women and their needs. The discussion questions are optional; the answers are provided to clarify my intent and stimulate your thought. You may have an entirely different insight as the Holy Spirit illumines your heart and mind.

Each section of the study has a specific purpose.

The *introductory paragraphs* furnish background information and lead in to the topic of that lesson.

The answers to the questions in *Section I* (Sounding the Depths of Your Heart) are personal and should not be discussed in the group. They will help prepare each woman's heart to receive God's Word as she does her own study.

Section II (In Light of the Scriptures) is aimed at studying the actual text of Scripture and understanding what it says.

The answers to the questions in *Section III* (Charting Your Course) should help to focus on various applications of the passage for that lesson.

Section IV (Drop Anchor) is not for group discussion. The suggested decisions are starting points for each lady to put God's truth into practice in her own life. You should close the session in prayer, asking God to bring lasting fruit from your study of His Word.

Section V (Stepping Out on Faith) will help to seal in your mind what you have learned from the passage.

The effectiveness of a group Bible study usually depends on two things: (1) the leader herself and (2) the ladies' commitment to prepare beforehand and interact during the study. You cannot totally control the second factor, but you have total control over the first one. These brief suggestions will help you be an effective Bible study leader.

You will want to prepare each lesson a week in advance. During the week, read supplemental material and look for illustrations in the everyday events of your life as well as in the lives of others.

Encourage the ladies in the Bible study to complete each lesson before the meeting itself. This preparation will make the discussion more interesting.

Also encourage the ladies to memorize the key verse or verses for each lesson. (The verse is printed below the title of each lesson.) If possible, print the verses on 3" x 5" cards to distribute each week. If you cannot do this, suggest that the ladies make their own cards and keep them in a prominent place throughout the week.

The physical setting in which you meet will have some bearing on the study itself. An informal circle of chairs, chairs around a table, someone's living room or family room—these types of settings encourage people to relax and participate. In addition to an informal setting, create an atmosphere in which ladies feel free to participate and be themselves.

During the discussion time, here are a few things to observe:

• Don't do all the talking. This is not designed to be a lecture.

• Encourage discussion on each question by adding ideas and questions.

• Don't discuss controversial issues that will divide the group. (Differences of opinion are healthy; divisions are not.)

• Don't allow one lady to dominate the discussion. Use statements such as these to draw others into the study: "Let's hear from someone on this side of the room" (the side opposite the dominant talker); "Let's hear from someone who has not shared yet today."

• Stay on the subject. The tendency toward tangents is always possible in a discussion. One of your responsibilities as the leader is to keep the group on the track.

• Don't get bogged down on a question that interests only one person.

You may want to use the last fifteen minutes of the scheduled time for prayer. If you have a large group of ladies, divide into smaller groups for prayer. You could call this the "Share and Care Time."

If you have a morning Bible study, encourage the ladies to go out for lunch with someone else from time to time. This is a good way to get acquainted with new ladies. Occasionally you could plan a time when ladies bring their own lunches or salads to share and eat together. These things help promote fellowship and friendship in the group.

The formats that follow are suggestions only. You can plan your own format, use one of these, or adapt one of these to your needs.

2-hour Bible Study

10:00—10:15 Coffee and fellowship time

10:15—10:30 Get-acquainted time

Have two ladies take five minutes each to tell something about themselves and their families.

Also use this time to make announcements and, if appropriate, take an offering for the babysitters.

10:30—11:45 Bible study
Leader guides discussion of the questions in the day's lesson.
11:45—12:00 Prayer time

2-hour Bible Study
10:00—10:45 Bible lesson
Leader teaches a lesson on the content of the material. No discussion during this time.
10:45—11:00 Coffee and fellowship
11:00—11:45 Discussion time
Divide into small groups with an appointed leader for each group. Discuss the questions in the day's lesson.
11:45—12:00 Prayer time

1¹/₂-hour Bible Study
10:00—10:30 Bible study
Leader guides discussion of half the questions in the day's lesson.
10:30—10:45 Coffee and fellowship
10:45—11:15 Bible study
Leader continues discussion of the questions in the day's lesson.
11:15—11:30 Prayer time

ANSWERS FOR LEADER'S USE

Information inside parentheses ( ) is additional instruction for the group leader. For additional information on Ephesians, consult a reliable Bible commentary, such as *The Bible Knowledge Commentary: New Testament Edition* by John F. Walvoord and Roy B. Zuck.

LESSON 1

Section II—1. Saints; the faithful in Christ Jesus. They would remind readers of their *position* in Christ as well as what their *practice* should be. ("Saints" are set-apart ones. They are people who have received Jesus Christ as their Savior; they are set apart unto God.)

2. Grace and peace.

3. He has blessed us with all spiritual blessings.

4. The blessings originate in "heavenly places" and "in Christ." This origin emphasizes that the blessings are supernatural and spiritual, not obtainable by human effort. A person must be "in Christ" to

receive them; a right relationship to Him is required.

5. He chose us to be in Christ; He predestined us to be adopted as His children through Jesus Christ.

6. Love; the good pleasure of His will; for the praise of the glory of His grace.

7. Redemption through His blood; the forgiveness of sins; the abounding grace of God.

8. All things in earth and in Heaven will be placed under the authority and rule of Christ.

9. To bring praise and glory to God.

10. We need to put our trust in Christ when we hear the words of the gospel. (See 1 Corinthians 15:1-4.) (*Ask:* What do the words "salvation" and "gospel" mean? Make sure the ladies in the group have a clear understanding of these terms.)

11. He gives us the Holy Spirit to dwell in us as a "seal" to guarantee our new relationship as God's children and our future inheritance. ("Sealing" was a familiar term in New Testament times. Sealing indicated ownership and security. Bancroft explains, "The Spirit is the signet seal of ownership which God places upon the life. He is the divine imprint and the pledge of the everlasting inheritance." The believer is "sealed" by the Holy Spirit at the moment of conversion.)

Section III—1. He is overwhelmingly gracious. He is eager to "adopt children" and pour great blessing on them. Since His focus is upon the good of these children, and since He is constantly alert to and caring for their needs, I should not be afraid or hesitant to go to Him for help. (*Discuss:* What is proper "fear" of God? Some people feel that God is not really good, that He doesn't want them to be happy. This causes fear. What does the Bible say about God's goodness? What about God should we "fear"?)

2. Personal answers. ("Adoption" places us into God's family as His children when we receive Christ as Savior. See Galatians 4:4, 5; John 1:12; 1 John 3:1.)

3. Personal answers. ("Redemption" has the idea to "purchase," or "buy in the marketplace." "Redemption" as it is used in relation to our salvation indicates that a payment had to be made; in this case, the blood of Christ. See Romans 3:24, 25 and 1 Peter 1:18, 19.)

4. "The inheritance is the kingdom of God with all its blessings" (*Baker's Dictionary of Theology*). We are now receiving many of the blessings of the inheritance; we will receive the inheritance fully when we are with Christ.

5. It was God's will and purpose to do it (vv. 5, 9, 11); He did it

because of His love and grace (vv. 4, 6, 7); He did it to bring praise and glory to Himself (vv. 6, 12, 14).

6. Personal answers.

7. The father was loving, giving, forgiving, gentle, compassionate, and patient.

8. The son was rejected by his brother and possibly by his "friends" when his money ran out.

9. Personal answers.

LESSON 2

Section II—1. Faith in Christ; love for other believers.

2. The spirit of wisdom and revelation. (Some commentators think this verse refers to the Holy Spirit, Who is the One Who imparts wisdom and revelation. Others would retain the small *s*, believing the verse to refer to the human attitude that seeks godly wisdom [insight into the true nature of things] and revelation [the "unveiling" of a subject; in this case, the knowledge of God]. If we accept the latter view, we recognize that it is the Holy Spirit Who enables the believer to have wisdom and revelation in regard to spiritual truths [John 16:13-15; 1 Cor. 2:9-14].)

3. They would have a knowledge of Him. (*Discuss:* Why is this a Biblical request? See Jeremiah 9:23, 24. What part does the Spirit have in helping us know God better? See John 16:12-15; Romans 8:15, 16; 1 Corinthians 2:10-12.)

4. The *hope* of His calling; the *riches* of the glory of His inheritance; the greatness of *His power* to us who believe.

5. It is primarily a spiritual perception that comes as a result of the Spirit's teaching. No doubt, coming to a new spiritual understanding of such deep truths can also affect a person's thoughts, emotions, and even bodily health.

6. Raised Christ from death; set Him in His exalted position at God's right hand.

7. He is far exalted above every power in the heavens and on earth, now and in the future. His is the only *real* power and influence.

8. He is the absolute authority and head of the church. The church and everything about it are subject to His control.

9. The church is His "body" on earth now that He is bodily in Heaven. It is joined to Him and does His bidding, just as the head directs the body to act.

10. We often think of Him in His suffering and humiliation, His lowly state during the crucifixion. Here He is presented as Lord of Lords, a King full of power and majesty.

Section III—1. It is foundational to all other truths. All truth comes from God, so in order to properly understand His words, we must understand His being and character. Also, the greater our concept of God, the greater our own spiritual perception will be. God Himself tells us to seek after a knowledge of Him (Jer. 9:23, 24; Prov. 9:10). We must remember that salvation isn't just about getting to Heaven; it is about a personal relationship with God and Jesus Christ (John 17:3). (*Discuss:* How will knowing God cause us to change our desire for power to the desire for humility instead?)

2. First of all you must recognize the importance of knowing God. Ask God to help you know Him better. This request is in His will (1 John 5:14, 15). Reading His Word is the primary source of learning about God. Each Old and New Testament book you read and study will deepen your knowledge of God. Always ask the Spirit to teach you as you read it. After reading a portion, ask yourself, "What does this passage teach me about God?" We may also read books by godly writers who explain to us the attributes of God. (Two good books to recommend are *Knowing God* by J. I. Packer and *The Knowledge of the Holy* by A. W. Tozer.)

3. *Hope*—Hope furnishes a goal. We already know the end of the story! We will be with Christ no matter what happens to us. This should cause us to persevere in all trials. *Riches*—God is willing to bless us spiritually and supply all spiritual needs. We should not be living like spiritual paupers, but joyful, well-supported daughters of the King! *Power*—God's infinite power is at work for and in us. Is there any need, any problem He can't handle? This truth should increase our faith. (*Discuss:* How does this type of praying exalt Christ and humble us?)

4. Christ's death, resurrection, and ascension assure us of the reality of this power. Without His victory over sin and death, how effective would a person's prayer for power be? It is the basis of our prayer's being answered. It also shows us the magnitude of this power.

5. Personal answers. (*Discuss:* How do we hinder God's power from working in our lives? Possible answers include sin, hard-heartedness, unbelief, self-sufficiency.)

6. Personal answers.

7. It is our job to bring glory to Christ, not to ourselves. A self-seeking attitude is an insult to our Savior. (*Discuss:* Does this mean a Christian should never seek to better his/her position in life? Should all opportunities for power, influence, and fame be shunned? The *key* is motivation. If God grants an opportunity to have influence or power

that can genuinely advance His cause in the world or in your life, it could be an acceptable position. If advancement is sought as a means of finding self-fulfillment and feeding pride, it would be unscriptural. Test question: Would I be *willing* to take a lower position in life if God called me to do it?)

8. Humility. This includes concern for others, not self; not striving after reputation, power, or control; being willing to serve; obedience to God's will above all else; trust in God for one's reward.

9. He is mightier than any other person, power, or force in the universe. Since we are His body, He will lovingly care for us as a person would his own body. Therefore, we know that He has both the desire and the ability to completely care for us.

10. Personal answers.

11. Himself (vv. 17-19); himself (v. 21); God and his soul (vv. 20, 21).

12. He wanted bigger, better, and more leisure, all to lavish on himself. He had no desire to know God, neither did he bother to find out what God wanted of him.

13. Knowing and doing the will of God.

14. In the end, he had nothing. He acted as if he were God, but found out that ultimately God had the final say in man's plans.

LESSON 3

Section II—1. She is "dead" (spiritually) because of her sins; she walks according to the course of the world; she is dominated by Satan (the "prince of the power of the air"); the spirit of disobedience works in her; she fulfills the lusts of the flesh and her mind; she is the object of God's wrath. (*Discuss:* Do you think unbelievers realize that these things are true of them? Does God try to tell them? See John 16:7-11. Why do most refuse to listen?)

2. "Quickened" you (made you spiritually alive); raised you up into heavenly places with Christ. That means He has given you a place in Heaven already. As far as He is concerned, you are already in Heaven along with Christ. Rich mercy, great love, and grace are the attributes of God from which we receive the benefits.

3. He wanted to demonstrate His abundant grace and loving-kindness as God. (Even the faith to believe comes from Him!) Verse 10 states that our purpose now, as God's children, is to do the "works" He has planned for us to do. God has a purpose for your life that He wants you to fulfill.

4. We are "made nigh" unto God; that is, we can approach Him and have a relationship with Him.

5. A wall no longer divides the two groups. Both are equally loved and accepted by God and have peace with Him.

6. We have access to the Father. As His daughters, we can come freely before His throne, without fear, to ask His help.

7. No longer foreigners, but citizens of God's country; members of God's household; part of a building being built by God.

8. Personal illustration. (*Discuss:* What is the purpose of a cornerstone? How does Christ Jesus fit this description? What is a foundation? How did the apostles and prophets fit this description?)

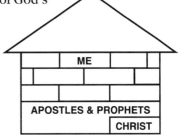

9. "Fitly framed together" by God's wisdom; growing; holy; the dwelling of God. This metaphor describes the church of Jesus Christ.

10. *Individuals*—to demonstrate His grace through all eternity; to have us do good works that will manifest "Christ in us." *Gentiles*—to give them a future hope and opportunity to share in the promises of God; to create a universal church, composed of all believers, Jew and Gentile. *Church*—the Holy Spirit dwells in both individual believers and the whole body of believers, creating a "temple" for God on earth.

Section III—1. Personal answers.

2. (a) Saved us. (b) Believed; asked God to save you. (c) Ask for it; believe that God will give it to you just as He gave you eternal life.

3. Personal answers.

4. We have been granted access to know God Himself (1 John 5:20) and the things of God (1 Cor. 2:10-12); we have access to God's power to work in us (2 Pet. 1:3-8); we have access to God in prayer (Heb. 4:16).

5. As citizens of Heaven, we need to conduct ourselves according to the laws and customs of God's country. Our daily lives should be focused on our eternal home with God; we are "foreigners" in this world. We should not be "at home" with the world's mindset and practices.

6. It is a place of safety/refuge; a place where needs are met; a place to be with family members; a place where one is instructed and given necessary information. In a household, each member has a responsibility to do his or her work, to follow the rules, to help and care for others, and not to bring disgrace upon the household.

7. You have an important place in the structure. You are needed to fill your position to assure the strength of those around you. If you

"fall away," you weaken the structure. We are all joined together "in Him." Therefore, you also need the other "bricks" to uphold you.

8. God has a place for you to fill in your local church. Your particular strengths and abilities are needed to minister His grace to others. You also need other people for your spiritual growth. (You may want to define the difference between the church, the Body of Christ, and its manifestation in the local church, if your ladies are not clear on this point.)

9. They made excuses for their failure to respond; they were too preoccupied with the things of this world and their own desires to respond to the invitation to come.

10. They were shown mercy; they were made to sit in the heavenly places with Christ; they were physical outcasts and had nothing in themselves to merit the privilege shown to them, just as we Gentiles were spiritual outcasts and were, by God's mercy, given the privilege of access to God.

LESSON 4

Section II—1. God's grace and power.

2. No.

3. The least of all the saints.

4. Yes; Paul was reliant on God's enabling to do it. No; there is no hint of feeling sorry for himself or excusing himself because he was "least."

5. Because of Christ's coming and atoning death, the Gentiles now have opportunity to become God's people, just as the Jews.

6. To preach the unsearchable riches of Christ to the Gentiles; to make known to everyone God's purpose in Christ.

7. (a) His manifold (multifaceted) wisdom; (b) the principalities and powers of Heaven. (*Discuss:* The Bible's definition of the church is the body of true believers in Jesus Christ; that is, people who have chosen to personally receive Him for eternal life and forgiveness of sins. The church is not a "religion" or a denomination. How does this definition of the church differ from the teaching of some religions and cults?)

8. (a) We have access to God; we can come boldly. (b) We can only come to the Father through Christ.

9. Praise, trust, boldness, willing to serve, caring about others.

10. Paul found joy and fulfillment in doing the work that God specifically had for him to do. He considered it a privilege to serve God; it gave meaning and direction to his life. (*Discuss:* Paul's main

ministry was to tell all people about the unsearchable riches of Christ. As Christians, this is our primary work for God too. What Scripture verses tell us that God wants all of us to witness about Christ? [Possible answers include Matthew 28:18–20; Acts 1:8; Romans 1:16.] What are some other things we can do for God that will bring us joy and purpose?)

Section III—1. All the works of our flesh (things we do in our own human strength and human ability) are tainted by sin (Rom. 7:18); therefore they cannot accomplish God's purposes. God's work must be done in His power and in His way (2 Thess. 2:16, 17; 2 Tim. 2:20, 21).

2. It exalts us rather than Him. Our good works are meant to point others to God's greatness, not our own greatness. (See Isaiah 48:11; Daniel 4:28–34; Colossians 3:17.)

3. Willingness to be used; dependence upon God's power; committing our abilities and gifts to His use for His glory.

4. Such a person is wrapped up in self and doesn't care about others. She is paralyzed by fear and often makes excuses for why she can't serve God.

5. An attitude of human insufficiency supposes that God's promises and power are not real.

6. Confess the sin of fear and self-centeredness; have an open heart to serve and be obedient to God's will; renew faith in God's power.

7. We are to present our bodies, ourselves, unto God as a living sacrifice, given over totally to Him for His use.

8. He preached and taught about Christ to all who came to his house; he had a mighty prayer ministry for others; he witnessed to the soldiers who guarded him until they all knew about Jesus; Paul's imprisonment made other believers bolder to witness; he wrote letters to believers to strengthen them. (Some of those letters are part of God's Word to us.)

9. We often react with self-centeredness, self-pity, fear, complaining, or even bitterness. Because our focus in hard times tends to shift to ourselves, we may cease to care about other people's needs, pray only about ourselves, lose our heart to seek God and serve Him. Note the difference between these reactions and Paul's responses. (*Discuss:* When problems hit and our energy levels are low, what steps can we take to keep from sliding spiritually? How can we continue to minister for God?)

10. Grace is the undeserved blessing, help, and kindness of God.

11. Grace is the source of enabling that works through our weak-

ness. God wants us to be totally dependent upon His power. (See 2 Corinthians 9:8.)

12. Personal answers.

13. The holiness of the church should reflect the holiness of God (1 Pet. 1:15); the love of the church demonstrates the love of Christ (John 13:34, 35); the glory of the church as it is united around the truth of God affirms the truth of Who Jesus Christ is (John 17:22, 23).

14. The world continually tells us to be number one. We are to overinflate our egos and decide there's nothing we can't do if we put our minds to it. The result is an attitude of independence, self-sufficiency, self-importance. In contrast, as believers we are able to look to God and Christ for everything. Does this tear down my self-respect? No, it raises it! If my self-concept is based on who I am, it will come crashing down when anything about me changes (I gain weight, get gray hairs, lose my job, etc.). But if my self-concept is founded on who I am in Jesus Christ, it should never change because He never changes. I exalt Him, and in Him I am exalted.This is the most secure position in the universe!

15. Bear fruit. "Fruit" is any service that accomplishes God's will on earth. For the Christian, her primary purpose on earth is doing God's will, not her own.

16. Abide in Christ; allow His Word to abide in us; continue in His love by obedience. (Note that the Lord does not put any conditions on being a fruitful branch, such as having an education or special abilities, having a good past, being in convenient circumstances, or feeling adequate for the job.)

17. Joy!

LESSON 5

Section II—1. Family.

2. We are called by Christ's name. (A more literal translation of the Greek is, "We are uniquely privileged to call God our Father.")

3. That Christ would dwell in their hearts by faith.

4. Through God's power as the Holy Spirit works in each believer's inner being.

5. Our whole relationship with God springs from His unconditional love for us. God's love reached out to us in our spiritual need and provided Christ's atoning death for the forgiveness of our sins and eternal life with Him. At the moment we placed our trust in Christ, we became recipients of God's love. Our spiritual roots were placed in the soil of His love, and daily we continue to grow in it.

6. The width, length, depth, and height of Christ's love.

7. Christ's love is infinite in all directions. (*Discuss*: Is it a contradiction to say that we can know something that surpasses knowledge?)

8. We will be filled with all the fullness of God.

9. This means we will be living an abundant, fulfilling, steadfast life in Christ.

10. He is able to do exceeding abundantly above all that we ask or think.

11. In us.

12. His power working in us.

13. Bring glory to Himself through believers' faith in Christ throughout all eternity.

Section III—1. *Galatians 2:20*—Because I am a believer, Jesus Christ will live out His life in me as I trust Him to do it. *John 15:5*—Daily I must live in a faith relationship with my Lord. Only through His power can I be fruitful for God. *1 Corinthians 1:30*—As Jesus Christ is free to live out His life in me, He becomes all I need: wisdom, righteousness, holiness, deliverance from sin's power. (You may want to discuss terms such as "abiding in Christ," "being filled with the Spirit," "walking in the Spirit." Basically they are synonymous, but there are variations of meaning. "Abiding in Christ" has the idea of maintaining unbroken fellowship with Him as we make our "home" with Him. The "filling of the Spirit" has to do with His control in our lives. And "walking in the Spirit" refers to living our daily lives in the awareness of His presence.)

2. This understanding enables you to serve with the focus on others, not yourself. You can't do anything that will make God love you more or less than He does now. Hence, you serve because you love God, not to make Him love you. Also, He continues to love you even when you don't do as well as you would like.

3. All of God's works are done in love, with the best interests of others in mind. If we are to reflect Christ's character, we must serve in love as Christ did. Love purifies our motives. (*Discuss:* What might be some of the wrong motives that prompt some Christians to "work" for God?)

4. God knows by our praying what is truly important to us. If spiritual growth is our goal, it will be a central part of our prayers. True progress will not be made unless we are asking God to work in ourselves and others.

5. That I may be strengthened by the Spirit's power in my inner being; that Christ may dwell in me today, His life flowing through me; that I may know the love of Christ for me; that I may be progressing

toward the fullness of God in my life; that I may not limit or hinder His power to work through me.

6. If Christians are not godly, vibrant in faith, and loving, we will not attract the attention of unbelievers. We will fail to be the kind of witnesses He directed us to be in Acts 1:8.

7. *Luke 1:15-20*—Zacharias *doubted God's ability* to give him a child because his wife was seemingly physically incapable of bearing a child. *Matthew 13:53-58*—The people of Nazareth admitted Jesus' wisdom and miracles, but because they knew his family, they logically couldn't accept Him as being the Messiah. Because they *couldn't understand,* they wouldn't believe or honor Him. Therefore He didn't do many works there. *Judges 6:1, 11-16*—Gideon doubted God's power and greatness because of *hardship* that had befallen his country. Also he viewed the poverty of his family and his place of *insignificance* as a hindrance to God's using him. God saw him as a man of valor based on what His power would do through him.

8. *1 Samuel 17:4, 32-37, 45, 46*—David trusted in God's power and name to enable him to defeat Goliath, the champion of the enemy. *Matthew 8:5-13*—The centurion believed that Jesus had the power to heal his servant, even from a far distance.

9. We may limit God's work in our lives by fear, doubt, pride, self-sufficiency, refusal to repent of sin.

LESSON 6

Section II—1. Live a life worthy of God's calling us to follow Christ.

2. Lowliness and meekness, longsuffering, forbearance, love, peace.

3. To "keep" the unity of the Spirit.

4. The Holy Spirit.

5. The Holy Spirit establishes the unity of a church. We are one because there is one body and one Spirit. As each of us lives a Spirit-filled life, we will act in accordance with the unity the Spirit has produced. The conduct outlined here will keep us in line with the unity of the church.

6. The "ones" are the doctrinal truths that bind us together. Those who have received Christ Jesus as personal Savior are Christ's body. We each have the Spirit of God; we share a future hope; we have one Lord—Jesus Christ; we were all saved by faith in His atoning death; we were baptized as a public sign of our relationship to Him; we are all true children of God. Unity is founded on these truths. Not everyone who calls herself a Christian believes these truths. Focusing on these truths will help us put verse 2 into practice.

7. Grace (v. 7) and gifts (v. 8).

8. Apostles, prophets, evangelists, pastor-teachers. "Apostle" in Greek means "messenger" or "ambassador." These were men by whose testimony and ministry Christ established His church (i.e., the disciples, Paul, and a few others). A prophet is a person who speaks God's words. Before the completion of the Bible, God spoke through chosen people in both the Old and New Testament eras (e.g., Jer. 2:1, 2; Acts 21:10, 11). According to Ephesians 2:19 and 20, both apostles and prophets were given to lay the church's foundation. Since that has been accomplished, these "gifts" are no longer needed. Hence, we do not have apostles or prophets in the strict Biblical meaning today. An evangelist is "one who announces good news." This is a person whose primary thrust is public preaching of the gospel so that people will be saved. (Acts 8:4–12 tells of Philip the evangelist.) Pastor-teachers are those who "shepherd the flock" (pastor) in a local church and "feed the sheep" (teach God's Word).

9. Leaders help the saints come to maturity and equip them so that they (the saints) can do the work of the ministry.

10. God's purpose is for us to be unified in the faith (doctrinal truths) and in the knowledge of Jesus Christ. In Christianity today, there is a movement to downplay doctrine and to emphasize a "unity" of love and extreme tolerance. True unity is founded on acceptance of clear, basic Bible truths. Also, this maturity of knowledge develops spiritual stability and helps us stay on God's true course for us. (*Discuss:* Of what kind of church must we be a part in order to develop the kind of maturity God wants for us? What might lead us to be "tossed . . . about with every wind of doctrine"?)

11. Speaking the truth in love.

12. Christ is causing the body to grow, but we are to be working out our part in making it grow. "Christ in you" (Col. 1:27) means Christ is working through us to carry out His work in the church.

Section III—1. Such a life continually seeks a deeper relationship with Christ and endeavors to serve Him faithfully. The believer's daily life should be filled with the Holy Spirit's power and grace, reflecting God's holiness and praise.

2. The qualities listed in verse 2 are Christ's qualities. Therefore, we must abide by faith in Christ to possess them. In our human efforts to demonstrate them, we may succeed for a while, but eventually we will fail. When we choose to yield to the Holy Spirit, He will give us grace to be godly people—even in sticky situations.

3. Unity is not just a warm, fuzzy feeling from being with a group of

people we enjoy. Biblical unity does not overlook sin and doctrinal error to avoid confrontation. But it does *not* mean people will always agree about everything. (It is about how they handle their disagreements!)

4. If a group of believers in a church are all in a right relationship to Jesus Christ and filled with the Holy Spirit, they will have a right relationship to each other. Verse 3 explains that unity is produced by the Spirit. Verse 2 explains that to maintain unity we must exhibit Christ's character. Verses 4-6 and 13 and 14 stress that unity is possible based only on common doctrinal agreement. Also, unity is effective as we focus on truly serving and edifying one another and unselfishly desiring God's work to go forward.

5. Personal Bible reading and Bible study are a must. Regularly attend services and Sunday School at a church where the Bible is faithfully preached and taught. Great books deal with every topic of Scripture, but be cautious in what you read and hear. Always compare men's words with the Scripture itself.

6. (a) Truth is that which is based on God's Word. (b) We speak in love when our main concern is the best interest of the person to whom we are speaking. We ought to attempt to be as tactful and sensitive as we can be, but, as the saying goes, sometimes "the truth hurts." (c) Speaking the truth in love is sometimes necessary because people are blind to their own sins and weaknesses. (d) In His Word, God continually assures us of His love, yet He frankly points out our sin and need. (e) Speaking the truth can sometimes be brutal. If the speaker is proud and unloving, the recipient will often see this and become bitter. Truth is not taken well from people who are themselves unspiritual. (f) Those who speak all love are often afraid of offending and being disliked. This is actually not love but selfishness. Love wants the other person to grow. (g) When someone speaks the truth in love to us, we should listen, examine our lives, ask God to show us if it is true and, if so, ask Him to change us. Whether speaking to someone or listening to someone, we should look to the Spirit's guidance to do what is right.

7. Personal answers.

8. They cared enough about his lack of knowledge to instruct him. They realized his potential to be used of God, that God had a place of ministry for him as well as for their friend Paul. They helped him mature in his knowledge of Christ.

9. Apollos was humble enough to receive their speaking the truth in love. As he matured, he used his gift of teaching to help the new converts grow as well.

10. Personal answers.

11. Personal answers.

LESSON 7

Section II—1. Vanity of the mind (synonyms are proud, empty, and valueless); their understanding is darkened (devoid of God's moral requirements); ignorant.

2. Blindness, or hardness, of heart.

3. Lascivious (lustful), unclean, greedy.

4. Our learning of Christ and Biblical truth.

5. Put off the old way of life; be renewed in the spirit of our mind; put on the new way of life in Christ.

6. (a) Deceitful lusts, or desires. (*Discuss:* Why are they called *deceitful* lusts?) (b) Righteousness and true holiness.

7. Lying.

8. Speak the truth. As believers, we are all members of one body.

9. We are not to sin.

10. "Let not the sun go down upon your wrath." Deal quickly with the situation that caused your anger. Be reconciled to the person with whom you are angry. Don't stew over it; you won't sleep well! "Neither give place to the devil." When we are angry with someone and don't deal properly with it, it opens us up to temptations from Satan to pull us deeper into sin: bitterness, gossip or slander, malice, etc. (*Discuss:* Think of all the ways that Satan can get a "foothold" by our anger.)

11. Labor; work constructively with hands; give to others in need. (*Discuss:* What is significant in Paul's telling the thief to give to those in need? How will this benefit the thief?)

12. Good, edifying, that which ministers grace. (*Discuss:* List all the ways that our speech can be corrupt.)

13. Bitterness, wrath, anger, clamor (fighting and arguing), evil speaking, malice.

14. Being kind, tenderhearted, forgiving.

15. God's loving and forgiving behavior toward us, as expressed through Christ.

Section III—1. Possible answers: any TV show or movie that presents sin as being acceptable; books with immorality; celebrities whose lives are ungodly; music that suggests improper sexual conduct; magazines that urge unbiblical feminism and inappropriate appearance/conduct.

2. *Lasciviousness*—The world says sex within a permanent, mo-

nogamous marriage is boring. Partners are "disposable" when we tire of the relationship or find someone more preferable. Don't limit yourself. <u>God says</u> sex only within a marriage; one woman with one man for as long as they both shall live. *Greed*—<u>The world says</u> get all you can; think of yourself first; money, things, power are everything. <u>God says</u>, "Seek ye first the kingdom of God, and his righteousness" (Matt. 6:33). *Deceitful lusts*—<u>The world says</u> don't deny yourself anything you want. <u>God says</u> He will supply all your needs and grant desires within His will; He knows what is best for you; be content with what you have.

3. Renewing our minds is the work of the Spirit and God's Word. We must read, study, meditate, and learn the truth of God in the Scriptures. We must also pray for God's work to take place in us.

4. The Holy Spirit creates holiness in us as we submit to Him and obey His leading. As we submit to Him, attend church, fellowship with godly believers, and put off "old life" habits, we will move toward Christlikeness.

5. Lying can be "little white lies," flattery, deceit, half-truths, hypocrisy. Lying should not be a part of a believer's life because God is truth, and we are to reflect His character (Deut. 32:4; John 14:6). Lying can hurt others and ruin our testimony for Christ.

6. Recognize that you are angry and try to figure out why. Often anger is the result of a *self* sin—someone hurts our ego, fails to meet our expectations, etc. Confess any sin. Don't mentally rehash the offense; talk to God. Think upon what might be a benefit or an explanation. If it was a true offense, humble yourself and commit it to God. He will give you grace to deal with your feelings. Commit it to Him as often as you are tempted to dwell on the irritation.

7. Stealing can be cheating, putting down wrong information or withholding information (such as on tax forms or financial statements), fixing time cards, taking company property, borrowing and not returning or repaying, taking someone's money when we can work ourselves, not trying to return found money or items, and many other such examples. Christians may justify stealing by feeling the government or company "owes" them; they're not hurting anyone; it's just a little thing.

8. Edifying, gracious speech can be praise, thanks, true compliments, teaching, encouraging, comforting, praying, etc.

9. Personal answers.

10. Jesus Himself said "salvation" had come to Zacchaeus' house and that Zacchaeus had become a "son of Abraham" (indicative of true faith).

11. Zacchaeus showed his commitment to Christ by his changed attitude and actions. Instead of getting, he now gave, and he was willing to make restitution fourfold to those he had wronged (v. 8).

12. The "old life" behaviors he left behind were stealing and lying, as well as greed.

LESSON 8

Section II—1. Be followers of God. We are His dear children.

2. Walk (live) in love. Christ loved us and gave Himself for us.

3. To give Himself up and offer Himself to God as a pleasing sacrifice. We can do the same by "dying" to ourselves and offering ourselves up to God to use as He pleases.

4. A saint is a person who has a relationship with God through repentance and faith in His Son. Therefore, he or she belongs to God, or is "set apart" unto God. Saints are to be separated *from* sin and separated *unto* God.

5. Fornication—sexual immorality; uncleanness—impurity of thought/behavior; covetousness—excessive desire; filthiness; foolish talk and jesting—includes vulgar and obscene language, off-color jokes, empty words that don't reflect God's views; whoremonger—a man who consorts with prostitutes; idolater—one who worships anything other than God.

6. The danger seemed to be that the believers were being deceived into thinking that such a lifestyle was fine for them because they were assured of Heaven. Paul reminded them that God judges these sins. Paul commanded them (in the literal Greek) to stop being partakers of the world's sin. Evidently, some were being enticed into sinful living.

7. In the Lord.

8. By being filled with the Spirit; by testing all things to see if they are acceptable to the Lord. (*Discuss:* How can we know what is acceptable to God? Stress the importance of knowing His Word.)

9. We are to reprove them. "Reprove" means "to rebuke, or censure." (*Discuss:* How can we reprove sin tactfully? Refer to "speaking the truth in love" in lesson 6.)

10. All sin will be exposed by God's light; we cannot hide sin.

11. A sleeper and a dead person.

12. Live carefully. Wisdom.

13. Not wasting any opportunity to live for God; trade our time for what is most valuable. We do this because the days are evil.

14. Understanding what God's will for us is.

15. The Holy Spirit.

16. (a) Psalms, hymns, spiritual songs. (b) In the heart. (c) The Lord.

17. Giving thanks for all things.

18. We will fear God and submit to others.

19. Fellowship.

Section III—1. (a) "Be ye followers of God" defines my focus, totally seeking after God's will and ways in my life. (b) "A sacrifice to God" tells the extent of my commitment: totally given over to God as His possession, reserving no part for myself. (c) "As becometh saints" sets the standards for my life and character. As a set-apart person, I should be pure, righteous, and holy.

2. (a) Loving as Christ did will assure that I always treat the other person according to his/her best interests. (b) I must be aware that there are teachers, philosophies, and ideas that can deceive me, and I must be wary of them. (c) All things must be tested to see if they are acceptable by God's Word. (d) Major decisions and actions should be prayed about until I understand what God's will is. (e) If I am filled with the Spirit, He will guide me into truth and show me what is good and righteous.

3. Possible answers: put God first in my life; read His Word; establish right priorities; have a good testimony for Christ; pray.

4. Possible answers: spend time with God and people; fulfill our responsibilities; serve God in ministries; witness; pray; learn; relax. Possible verses are Psalms 39:4; 90:10, 12; James 4:14, 15.

5. Confess all known sin (1 John 1:9); by faith ask God to fill you and believe you are filled (Luke 11:13, 1 John 5:14, 15); yield yourself to His power and work in you, and obey as He leads (Eph. 4:30).

6. Simon needed to put off covetousness and idolatry as well as bitterness and sin's bondage.

7. Peter reproved the works of darkness and did not partake of them.

8. The new believers in Acts 19 exposed their sin to the light (confessed). They discerned what was acceptable to God and got rid of what dishonored Him.

LESSON 9

Section II—1. (a) A willingness to submit ourselves to them. (b) The Holy Spirit fills and enables us.

2. (a) The fear of God. (b) When we fear, or truly reverence, God, we desire to please Him in any way He directs us.

3. Submission is linked to love and unity (v. 2); strife and pride do away

with submission. Humility will cause us to consider the needs of the other person as being more important than our own needs (vv. 3, 4).

4. We consider the other person as being more important than ourselves; therefore we act in love and harmony with that person. Submission, really, is giving way to the other person and allowing him or her respect above ourselves. (*Discuss:* To many people, the word "submission" suggests becoming an unthinking, silent doormat. Does submission mean going along with everything? When should we keep silent and when should we speak up? What attitudes are important in strained relationships?)

5. To the Lord and also to her husband. Submitting to the Lord will enable her to properly submit to her husband.

6. God has placed the husband in a position of authority over the wife.

7. The church is under Christ's authority just as a wife is under her husband's authority. (*Discuss:* Some women rebel against these verses because they mistakenly think that the verses teach inequality of women and men. Is Jesus Christ inferior to God? Does He submit to God? What does Christ's example teach us as women? See Galatians 3:28, 29; 1 Corinthians 11:3, 11, 12. Why is this plan of "subjection" necessary? There is a whole order of subjection in the universe. Read Hebrews 1:1—2:9. The "two masters" system just doesn't work! See Luke 16:13.)

8. Love (vv. 25, 28); give (v. 25); sanctify and cleanse (v. 26); present (v. 27); nourish, cherish (v. 29). (*Discuss:* How will each of these actions by a husband enhance his relationship with his wife?)

9. They are to merge all aspects of their lives together. In God's eyes they are inseparably joined. It is as if they are now *one* person.

10. The husband and wife are to leave behind their dependence (physical, mental, and emotional) upon their parents. They establish a new family before God. The husband is to be devoted to his wife's well-being, and the wife is to look to her husband for the provision of her needs and help in making decisions. (*Discuss:* What problems can arise when a husband or wife fails to leave, physically and mentally, his or her parents? What is a proper relationship to his and her parents after marriage?)

11. Reverence. It means to regard with honor and respect, especially with tenderness of feeling.

12. Obey and honor.

13. It may be well with you; you will live long in the land. It might show the importance of the command or the daily difficulty of carrying out the command.

14. They should not provoke their children to anger. They should train up children in the nurture and admonition of the Lord. (*Discuss:* Look up "nurture" and "admonition." As her husband's helpmeet, how can a mom enhance her children's spiritual growth?)

15. Willingness to obey (v. 5); fear and trembling (v. 5; this denotes respect for authority and a realization of accountability); singleness of heart (v. 5; diligence); not with eye service (v. 6); from the heart (v. 6; sincerely); with good will (v. 7; work cheerfully).

16. We are servants of Christ; we want to do God's will; we will be rewarded by our heavenly Master.

17. They are to be mindful of their service to Christ. They should not threaten, but practice forbearance. All people—including servants—are treated fairly by God.

Section III—1. Answers include pride, bitterness, worry, fear.

2. *Love*—A wife should love her husband and show respect for him; build him up; keep an attractive appearance and a sense of humor; don't nag and complain. *Give of himself*—Express gratitude; show an interest in his interests; show him she wants to be with him. *Sanctify*—Share on a spiritual level as much as possible; ask him his opinions on Biblical matters; pray with him and for him as a spiritual leader of the home. *Nourish*—Her husband should know she needs him; ask his advice on matters and share ideas and concerns; don't be independent of each other, but one. *Cherish*—Be a valuable helpmeet to her husband; be wise, supportive, fun, and sensitive to his needs; be his friend!

3. *Thoughts and attitudes*—Continually dwell on his good qualities and why she came to love him; think of his potential in Christ and how he will grow by her prayers; be free from bitterness for past offenses; be grateful for all his kind deeds. *Words*—Don't tear him down, but build him up; thank him; compliment him; talk to him about concerns and opinions. *Actions*—Do acts of kindness for him, especially when he is tired; do things with him when possible.

4. She should respect his position as her husband. Express genuine gratitude for anything he does that is praiseworthy. (Sometimes husbands feel like failures because they know their wives don't respect them.) Be sure to pray for him, but refrain from nagging him or tearing him down. Communicate with love.

5. You can go to them for counsel; take time to keep in touch with them; express thanks to them for all they have done for you; care for their needs as well as you can.

6. Personal answers.

7. (a) Abram offered Lot first choice of the land. (b) God exalted

Abram and blessed him with land and descendants. (c) Abram made an altar to God.

8. (a) Hannah didn't nag or blame her husband; she didn't act with resentment or bitterness but went with him to worship the Lord. (b) She showed strength by taking her concerns to God, by leaving her troubles with God and trusting Him to work them out. Also, she formulated a plan for raising Samuel, shared it with her husband, and carried it out. (c) Hannah's godly attitudes motivated Elkanah to love and cherish her (vv. 5, 8), to give freely to her (v. 5), to nourish her (vv. 8, 22, 23).

9. Jesus, though in great anguish, felt the concern of His mother's care. He appointed a trusted friend to care for her needs.

10. The servant obviously loved his master and wanted to please him and carry out his request. He sought God's help to fulfill his responsibility.

11. There was an air of good will between Boaz and his workers. He cared for them. They apparently regarded him highly. How many employees ask God to bless their employer?

LESSON 10

Section II—1. Be strong in the Lord and in His mighty power; put on the whole armor of God.

2. The Devil (v. 11), who is wily (crafty, beguiling); principalities, powers, rulers of darkness and wickedness (v. 12). Though the distinctions among these demons are not clear, the titles suggest a well-organized system of attack on Satan's part. The Greek word for "high places" can be translated "the heavenlies." This brings to mind Ephesians 2:2, where Satan is described as "the prince of the power of the air." Here is a supernatural army of wickedness!

3. All believers, including me!

4. Stand and withstand. (*Discuss:* How are these two actions different?)

5. Gird your loins with truth. (Think of the word "girdle," a support garment!) The loins are between the ribs and hips. In ancient days, the long, flowing robe had to be girded in order for the wearer to move with ease.

6. The truth.

7. If we aren't supported by God's truth, we will get all tangled up and fail almost immediately. We need to know the Bible truths on which we stand, otherwise Satan can effectively bring us down by wrong thoughts and attitudes and resulting emotions.

8. The breastplate of righteousness. It covered the vital organs, such as the heart and lungs.

9. Satan is the accuser of believers. Christ's righteousness, that which covers us before God, is our defense. Secondly, living righteously in Christ's power protects us from many snares in life.

10. Our feet being shod, or protected, by the gospel of peace.

11. The gospel is the "good news" of Jesus Christ's death, burial, and resurrection.

12. When we have believed the gospel and know God is for us, we can have inward peace and security in life's trials. (See Isaiah 26:3; Romans 8:37-39.)

13. The shield of faith. It is needed to quench all the fiery darts of Satan.

14. The helmet of salvation.

15. When we become new creations in Christ, our thinking and attitudes are "made new." We think about life from God's perspective instead of from Satan's and the world's.

16. The Sword of the Spirit (the Bible) and prayer.

17. As a defensive weapon, God's promises and truth protect us from Satan's lies and doubts. As an offensive weapon, with the light of God's Word, we fight off the darkness. We strengthen God's realm as we bring others to Christ by the presentation of His Word (Rom. 10:17).

18. Pray always; pray for self and others; pray in the Spirit; prayer is spiritual watching (be alert to the enemy's movements); prayer takes perseverance; all saints need my prayers.

19. To speak the gospel boldly.

20. Peace, love, faith; through God's grace and sincere love for Jesus Christ.

Section III—1. He desires to destroy us spiritually so that we will be out of fellowship with God and ineffective witnesses for Christ.

2. Possible answers include these ideas: Satan wants us to doubt God's goodness (God is unfair and doesn't want us to enjoy what is best in life); he wants us to think God doesn't love us or that, because of our failure, we can't ever please God. (The truth is that God totally loves and accepts us in Christ. Though we fail, He gives us grace to grow and go on.)

3. Possible answers: I have to try harder; I don't have enough faith; I'll never be able to be a good Christian.

4. We put on the armor by reading God's Word and meditating on it; by reminding ourselves of God's truth as thoughts, attitudes, feelings arise in various temptations and circumstances; by praying daily (especially in the morning) for cleansing from sin through

Christ's blood; by continuing to meditate, pray, and respond to the Holy Spirit's leading as we go through our day.

5. Personal answers.

6. *Peace*—Tychicus comforted others, which is only possible if one is full of trust and peace. *Love*—He was a beloved brother; God's people loved him. *Faith*—He faithfully ministered for the Lord.

7. Personal answers.